RMS QUEEN ELIZABETH

The Beautiful Lady

Janette McCutcheon

AMBERLEY

To Barbara from
John

Christmas 2016

Cunard's *Queen Elizabeth* was one of those liners that almost, but not quite, managed to survive to preservation. Today, she has been lost forever and survives only in the memory of those who worked and travelled aboard her, and in books such as this. This book should not be looked upon as a definitive history of the ship, but as a visual record of one of the finest liners ever to sail. The *Lizzie*, as she was affectionately known, still evokes happy memories for many thousands. I hope this book does too!

First published 2002, this revised edition 2014

Amberley Publishing
The Hill, Stroud
Gloucestershire, GL5 4EP

www.amberley-books.com

ISBN 978 1 4456 3804 1 (print)
ISBN 978 1 4456 3823 2 (ebook)

British Library Cataloguing in Publication Data.
A catalogue record for this book is available from the British Library.

Typeset in 11pt on 12pt Sabon LT Std.
Typesetting by Amberley Publishing.
Printed in the UK.

Cunard

THE SUPERLINER WAY
TO and FROM
EUROPE

QUEEN MARY   QUEEN ELIZABETH

CUNARD

Europe to all America

R.M.S QUEEN MARY
ARRIVING AT
NEW YORK

R.M.S QUEEN ELIZABETH
LEAVING THE OCEAN
TERMINAL, SOUTHAMPTON

FASTEST OCEAN SERVICE IN THE WORLD

Cunard's *Bothnia* illustrated on an 1870s advertising trade card.

Lucania at Liverpool, *c.* 1900.

An Odin Rosenvinge advert for Cunard's emigrant service.

CHAPTER ONE

CUNARD, THE
EARLY YEARS

RMS *Campania*, a Cunard Blue Riband winner at Liverpool *c.* 1900. She lasted in service until 1914, was sold to the Admiralty and converted into a seaplane carrier, sinking in 1918 in the Firth of Forth.

On 9 January 1972 a Queen lay dying in Hong Kong harbour. Fires blazed in her public rooms, smoke billowed from her portholes and fireboats milled round like ants spraying water on her in an effort to control the blazes aboard. The regal *Queen Elizabeth*, the one-time largest ocean liner in the world and pride of the Cunard fleet, caught fire and keeled over whilst being converted to a floating university and cruise ship. This was a far cry from the dreams of Samuel Cunard, founder of the Cunard Line.

Samuel Cunard was born in Halifax in 1787 and made his fortune through such diverse trades as banking, lumber and whaling. His company obtained the British government contract to transport mail between Boston, Halifax, Bermuda and Newfoundland. Cunard then set his sights on the lucrative mail contract between Britain and North America. This was at a time when steamships were still relatively rare on the North Atlantic, and the government contract called for a regular and, most importantly, reliable service. In order to do this, he needed to have a fleet of ships that were capable of transporting the mails speedily and efficiently. He approached Robert Napier, a shipbuilder and engineer on the Clyde, and started a long tradition of having Cunard ships constructed on Clydeside. Napier designed the steamship *Britannia*, the first of a long line of famous Cunarders. Compared to the giant Queens, *Britannia* was tiny – she was only 1,154 tons, 207ft long and 34ft 6in wide. *Britannia* left the Clyde on 12 June and headed for Liverpool. Little fuss was made of her when she arrived at Coburg Dock. After all, she was smaller than the 1838 *Great Western* and her arrival attracted only two lines in the local press. *Britannia* left Liverpool at 2 p.m. on Saturday 4 July 1840 with only sixty or so passengers on board, including Samuel Cunard and his daughter Ann. Eleven days and four hours later she arrived at Halifax to a gun salute from HMS *Winchester*. On 19 July she arrived in Boston to another great reception, with the USN cutter *Hamilton* escorting her in, and more salutes from shore batteries.

After this initial success, Cunard added new ships to his fleet – *Caledonia*, *Arcadia* and *Columbia*. The four ships could guarantee a regular service as mail packets, for which the company received a large subsidy, and the carrying of passengers was secondary on these early vessels. However, with their reliability and guaranteed arrival and departure dates, the ships soon became profitable as passenger vessels. Cunard applied a simple rule to their vessels, and safety, not excessive speed in dangerous conditions or luxury, was paramount. As traffic on the North Atlantic increased, other companies began to enter the burgeoning market and followed Cunard's example. Passenger numbers were increasing rapidly and soon more and more luxurious and faster ships were being designed. These ships carried the cream of the passenger trade – people for whom money was no object. Cunard still followed their basic principle – safety first, not luxury – and the ships were plainer than most, but every effort was made to ensure they arrived safely. Other companies, more concerned with profit and speed, compromised this basic principle with disastrous results.

DISASTER

Edward Collins was one of Cunard's main rivals. His company, the Collins Line, was subsidised by the American government, and he had built luxurious and fast ships, which took away some trade from Cunard. The accommodation and cuisine on board were equivalent to that offered by the premier hotels of London, New York and Paris. The ships were fast but safety was much lower on the agenda. In 1852 Collins Line ships carried more passengers than the Cunarders, but they did not have the advantage of a large Royal Mail subsidy, and their ships, fast as they were, were not as economical to run. The misfortunes of the Collins Line really started in 1854 when the *Arctic* collided with another steamer and sank, taking most of the passengers to their deaths. As a double blow, Collins' wife and daughter were on board *Arctic* and were drowned in the tragedy. Only eighteen months later, 186 passengers and crew on another Collins liner, the *Pacific*, disappeared without trace. With high running costs, the loss of two ships in quick succession and high labour costs, the company went bankrupt in 1856.

Another unfortunate competitor was White Star – owners of the three sisters – *Titanic*, *Olympic* and *Britannic*. In 1871 the White Star company brought ocean liner travel literally screaming into a new age with the introduction of their new transatlantic steamships, *Oceanic*, *Atlantic*, *Baltic* and *Republic*. These new ships, from a potent new force in Atlantic travel, introduced unheard of luxuries to first-class passengers, which

A postcard view of a ship on Cunard's Canadian service. Originally owned by Thomson Line, Cunard purchased this route in 1910.

would never be expected on a ship. Introductions by the White Star Line included central heating, electric lighting and baths. Unfortunately, White Star suffered more than its fair share of casualties. The *Atlantic* sank in 1873 off the Canadian coast, after running low on coal, with the loss of 585 passengers and crew, the *Naronic* disappeared without trace in 1893, the *Republic* sank in 1909 after being rammed – her passengers and crew being rescued in the first use of radio by a ship in distress, the *Olympic* collided with HMS *Hawke* off the Isle of Wight in 1911 and the *Britannic* was torpedoed in 1916 while on war service in the Aegean. The worst disaster, and the best known of all shipping disasters, was the loss of the luxury 'unsinkable' liner, *Titanic*, in April 1912. She carried the minimum number of lifeboats as decided by the British Board of

Trade but they had room for only half her passengers and crew. When she struck an iceberg late at night on 14 April 1912 some of the lifeboats were despatched only partly filled. As the passengers and crew exceeded the available spaces onboard the lifeboats a lot of people drowned unnecessarily. The Atlantic was freezing cold and it took an average of six minutes to die. After the *Titanic* disaster, maritime law was changed in order that all ships should carry enough lifeboats for all passengers and crew; and that there should be a lifeboat drill for everyone just after sailing. These have grown to encompass the SOLAS (Safety of Life at Sea) regulations that control safety on merchant ships today.

THE GREAT ATLANTIC RACE

More people and therefore more and bigger ships were crossing the Atlantic regularly, and the period from the 1850s saw the founding of many of the great steamship companies. Businessmen found that the burgeoning economies of America and Canada were opening up new opportunities for both exports and imports. Some people just wanted a new life and emigrated to America to escape privations and hardships or political and religious persecution at home. The possible opportunities also lured people to the new world. Quite often, family and even extended family would make the trip too and the numbers were growing every year.

To cope with the sheer volume of traffic, shipping lines were building bigger and more luxurious ships. Ship sizes had grown since 1840 and the modern liner of 1901 was probably 18,000 tons and could carry around 2,600 passengers at sixteen knots as well as 3,000–5,000 tons of cargo. As time progressed, the technology was becoming more advanced and the ships, although larger, were becoming faster and more fuel-efficient.

The fastest and most luxurious ships attracted the finest clientele. The rich and famous had two reasons for travelling on the fastest ships: one was to get to their destination quicker and the second was simply to be seen and to travel in style on the fastest ship. The poorer emigrants also travelled on the faster ships, after all they were leaving literally on a trip of a lifetime and the small extra cost of the 'better quality' ships was of little consideration for those who could afford it. Many of the poorer people aspired to be like their counterparts in the first-class section, so they often chose a ship that reflected their hopes and aspirations. Maybe a first-class ticket was out of reach, but you could send home a postcard showing the luxurious first-class section of the fastest and most luxurious liner in the world! It was soon fashionable to cross the Atlantic on the speediest ship. After all, a trip of six or seven days was not just about eating and sleeping. Networking and meeting other business people and politicians was a very important use of time on board and many people travelled for this reason on the best ships. For the ships on the Atlantic route the Blue Riband was given for the speediest journey from Ambrose Light in America to Bishop's Rock, England. For the company with the fastest crossing came the cream of the traffic. Speed was everything, and in the same way that Concorde attracted the most important people, the fastest liners attracted the finest customers.

Shipping lines started to compete for the fastest crossing from Europe to America and, for a period at the end of the nineteenth century, the German lines came to the fore. In 1897, the North German Lloyd *Kaiser Wilhelm der Grosse* sped across the Atlantic, taking the Blue Riband for Germany. Then, in 1900, *Deutschland* took the prize for Hamburg-Amerika with a speed of 22.4 knots.

Two years later, John Pierpoint Morgan, an American financier who had made his money in banking, started buying up shipping lines. His new company was called International Mercantile Marine (IMM) and his aim was to monopolise the trade on the North Atlantic. The idea was that IMM could operate a cartel of lines and begin to charge higher

Top left: The ill-fated RMS *Lusitania*, winner of the Blue Riband in 1907, was tragically sunk by U-20, a German U-boat, in May 1915.

Above: Saxonia at speed in the Mersey.

Bottom left: Ascania, one of the Canadian steamers.

Top right: The Second Cabin Dining Saloon, RMS *Aquitania*, 1914.

Above: Aquitania enters the water in 1913, after her launch at John Brown's on Clydeside.

Bottom right: Aquitania in Southampton's floating dry dock, *c.* 1925, for her annual refit.

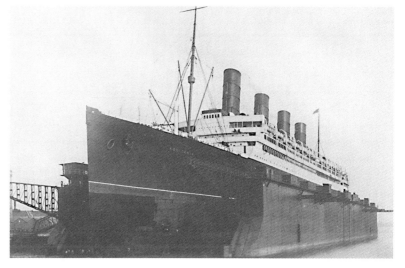

fares thereby making a fortune in profits. IMM owned or purchased such companies as the American Line, Atlantic Transport Line, Dominion Line, Frederick Leyland and Red Star Line, then became the largest shareholder in the White Star Line. This made the British government uneasy as White Star and Cunard were the two biggest companies that could supply troopship transports in the event of a war. The British government only allowed IMM to become the largest shareholder of the White Star Line if the ships remained under the British flag and had British crew. IMM agreed – after all it suited them anyway, British taxes and dues were less than in other countries, and to sail ships under the American flag was prohibitively expensive and the regulations of ownership stricter.

Then IMM upset the government by making an offer for the Cunard Line. The offer was refused and in 1903 the British government signed a twenty-year agreement with Cunard to finance two record-breaking superliners with troopship capacity. Cunard was subsidised to the tune of £150,000 per annum to ensure their ships could be available at short notice for Admiralty use. It wasn't the first time that the government had considered the problem of troopships. During the Crimean War most of the Cunard fleet had been called up for war service. In 1885 the British Admiralty also set up a committee to look into subsidising merchant ships that could be converted into troop carriers, and many were used during the Boer War for this purpose.

The main points of the Admiralty contract were: two new ships were to be built capable of maintaining a speed of 24.5 knots and £2,600,000 was loaned to pay for construction; the Cunard company was to remain British; no major investment was allowed from any foreign line or company; and both ships were to be capable of being converted into troopships if the British government required them. They were to become the *Mauretania* and *Lusitania*.

Britain, having won the Blue Riband many times over the years, again became a major contender in the race to America. While the Cunard company was more concerned with safety first, they did now have the fastest liners in the world. The company's official attitude to the prestigious award was that winning it would be nice but not necessary. Their unofficial attitude must have been one of pride in having the fastest vessels in the world. Certainly, publicity was geared towards the fact that Britain, and Cunard, held the Blue Riband.

As news was released out about the two new Cunarders, other companies began to plan new liners. White Star started construction of *Titanic* and *Olympic* just after the Cunarders entered service, and then the Hamburg-Amerika Line answered, with the *Imperator*, *Vaterland* and *Bismarck* all launched between 1912 and 1914.

Mauretania and *Lusitania* were built at Swan, Hunter & Wigham Richardson on the Tyne, and John Brown's on the Clyde respectively and were the pride of the British merchant fleet at the time of construction. Both held the Blue Riband for a period, with *Mauretania* holding the record until the late 1920s. Unfortunately, *Lusitania* was sunk off the Old Head of Kinsale by a German U-boat with the loss of over 1,000 passengers and crew. At the end of the war she was replaced in the Cunard fleet by the German ship *Imperator* as part of the war reparation scheme. In 1921 *Imperator* was renamed and became Cunard Line's *Berengaria*.

A third superliner was to join *Mauretania* and *Lusitania* just before war started in 1914 – she was the *Aquitania* and she made three journeys before war started. The *Aquitania* was also built at John Brown's and not only was she the last four-funnelled transatlantic liner built but she was the only four stacker to have served in both world wars. The First World War saw a great change in the make-up of the national shipping lines. Many ships were sunk and, at the end of the war, many of the remaining German ships were acquired by Allied shipping lines.

Above right and right: Mauretania, the fastest liner in the world for over twenty years, sees war service in 1916 and makes her way to the breaker's yard in 1935.

Top left and above: Berengaria being painted and in dry dock.

Aquitania in Southampton, 1938.

CHAPTER TWO

THE FIRST GREAT QUEEN OF THE ATLANTIC

By 1926, the *Aquitania*, *Mauretania* and *Berengaria* were becoming past their best and the Germans and Italians were building new modern ships to replace the ones lost by war. The French had been building too and *Île de France*, *Lafayette* and *Paris* were either finished, on the stocks or at the planning stage. Rumours were intimated that the French were also planning a new superliner that would be faster and more beautiful than any ship afloat.

Passenger numbers were, however, falling on the Atlantic, and Cunard was looking at ways of cutting costs. As technology moved forward, a more economic solution to providing a regular weekly service had to be found by Cunard. The most viable solution would be to have two new liners. In calculating this, the new liners had to be capable of maintaining a 30-knot speed in moderate weather. Two liners were more economical than three because the expenditure was less – cutting down on food bills, wages, fuel bills and docking charges. By 1926, Cunard was already making plans for the first ship. In utter secrecy, naval architects were designing the ship to suit Cunard's requirements, schedules of sailing were being calculated with 'turn-around' times – the minimum amount of time taken for the ship to unload, replenish stocks and then reload – and discussions were taking place with ports in New York and Southampton regarding extending piers and dredging channels for the new superliners. After the design details were finalised, model ships were made and floated in massive tanks in order to assess the dynamics of the ship in all weathers and streamline the exterior design.

John Brown's on the Clyde were pleased to receive notification on 28 May 1930 that they had won the contract to build the new British superliner. She was given a temporary name of Hull 534 – as she was the 534th vessel to be built in the yard. 534 created a whole new set of problems for Cunard and her builders. Special insurance had to be sought because no one had insured an object this large or this costly

PS *Kylemore* passes the hull of 534 on the stocks at John Brown's yard in Clydebank, 1934. The hull of 534 remained here from 1931 to 1934 after a shutdown of work due to the Depression. She was so well looked after on the stocks that, beyond cleaning of surface rust and bird droppings, work restarted almost immediately.

before and then there was the problem of a dry dock at Southampton. The Southern Railway, owners of the site that the new dry dock was to be built on, didn't want to build a dry dock for just one ship. They already had a floating dry dock that could cope with the largest liners then in service. After much negotiation and gentle persuasion from the government, it was agreed that the new dry dock would be built. On 26 July 1933, Their Majesties King George V and Queen Mary sailed into the new dock in their Royal Yacht, *Victoria and Albert*.

After the announcement in May 1930 about the 534, Clydebank and John Brown's became alive with excitement about the new liner. On

1 December 1930 the first keel plate was laid and by the end of January 1931, the entire keel had been laid out and extended for almost 1,000ft down the slipway. At the end of November 1931, 80 per cent of the hull plating was in place, and steel, castings and mechanical parts for the new ship were coming from all over the country to Clydebank.

A black cloud had been looming on the horizon – the world was in the grip of the Great Depression and the financial outlook seemed bleak. The state of the world economy was precarious to say the least, huge losses were made on Wall Street and in London's Stock Exchange, and in turn, many personal fortunes collapsed. People were travelling less and in cheaper classes of accommodation, fewer emigrants were being allowed into the United States and trade was drastically down on the Atlantic. Some people could not afford to travel at all. Cunard was feeling the pinch and its profits dried up. In December 1931 the company took the decision to suspend work on the new liner as profits and cash reserves were dwindling. The future looked bleak for 534. Then, on 11 December 1931, work was halted on 534, having a disastrous effect on the economy of not only Clydebank but of the whole country. The ship, the largest under construction, employed thousands at Clydebank alone, as well as tens of thousands elsewhere in the UK supplying steel, engines, motors, castings, wood, china, silverware, artwork, furniture and linen. The men made redundant on Clydeside had little money to survive on. Many children went to school unfed and with clothes in tatters. Few had money to spend in local shops and pubs. Reverberations were felt throughout the country because hundreds of firms relied on orders for 534 – from machinery to furniture, from wine glasses to medical equipment, the cost to the economy of losing these orders was huge. Almost every industry in Britain was affected by the stoppage on 534 – many employees of these firms were laid off because there was no

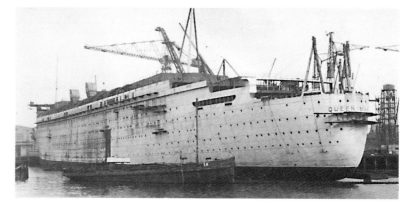

Top: Now named *Queen Mary*, the hull is in the water at last.

Above: In the fitting-out basin, her name has been added to her cruiser stern. She was painted a light grey for launching to enable the many photographers to get a better image of her. The lighter at her stern was there to prevent damage from the many ships sailing up and down the river.

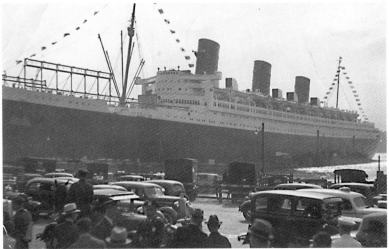

Above left: Queen Mary travels down the Clyde from the shipyard in March 1936.

Left: Arriving in New York, June 1936 on her maiden voyage.

Above: A First Class bedroom.

work. The knock-on effect of the direct and indirect job losses was huge. Such was the concern in Clydebank that the local MP David Kirkwood took up the case. He lobbied both the government and Cunard, and even spoke to the Prince of Wales about the situation. He was convinced that if the construction of 534 was restarted, it could give the British economy the kick-start needed to help regenerate it. If the French government could subsidise the building of the new French superliner, why couldn't the British government help their shipbuilding industry?

Above: Queen Mary's third-class smoking room.

Above left: Cabin suite sitting room.

The government was wary. The days of subsidising shipping lines were over. On one hand, it would be useful to kick-start areas of the economy by lending money to complete 534, but on the other, people may see this as a frivolous waste of money – building a new high-class liner when there was no money and no work. In the end the government used the dilemma as a way of solving a problem by agreeing to loan the money to fund the building only if a merger of Cunard and the other major British line, White Star, was undertaken. White Star had major financial problems. It had just been split from the Royal Mail Lines group of companies after the latter had gone bust. It was short of money, had antiquated liners and would also need a subsidy to survive. The prospect of having to subsidise two lines with too much combined tonnage was unacceptable for the government and a merger was a neat solution for them. The British government also ensured that both lines stayed British and that the combined shipping could be relied upon in time of war. Therefore, the government wanted the merger to ensure an equally strong position for Cunard and White Star. The government decided it would provide a loan for 534, as well as one for her proposed sister ship. It would also provide some working capital, in return for the merger. The loan agreement went to Parliament and was passed as the North Atlantic Shipping (Advances) Bill on 27 March 1934.

Within a few days a simple letter popped through the door of hundreds of ex-employees at John Brown's. It said, 'Dear Sir, please report to Messrs John Brown & Co. Ltd, Clydebank, on Tuesday April 3, 1934 at 7.40 a.m., ready to start work. Please hand the enclosed introduction card to employer.' Clydeside was ecstatic! Workers were marched into the yard by pipe bands, and the whole community turned out to see this wonderful sight. The shipyard workers started to scramble over the huge hull like ants, the ship was cleaned of bird droppings (it had been so well cared for during the work stoppage that there was no problem in starting the work again), orders were placed and parts started flooding in from all over the country.

Hull 534 was ready for launch on 26 September 1934. Queen Mary herself launched the great liner with a bottle of Australian Chardonnay (French champagne was deemed inappropriate). The new 81,000-ton liner was named *Queen Mary* and was called 'Britain's Masterpiece' in the special publicity issued for her launch and maiden voyage.

The *Queen Mary*, although very art deco and exquisitely decorated, was a more homely ship than her French opposition – the *Normandie*. The *Normandie* was full of the best of French artwork, had one of the finest restaurants afloat and was very ostentatious, whereas the *Queen Mary* was more down to earth and, as a result, more welcoming.

As in France, Cunard used well-known national artists to design the public rooms. Artists included Doris and Anna Zinkeisen and Dame Laura Knight, and only the best materials were used on board – it was boasted in one particular promotional booklet on the *Queen Mary* that she had over thirty different types of wood on board. The new *Queen* had the most up-to-date ballroom lighting installation and gymnasium equipment. The children's playroom could even boast a tropical fish tank and a chute!

Queen Mary inspired a nation, and it seemed as if they all cheered as she sailed on her maiden voyage on 27 May 1936. She deserved the accolade and was truly 'Britain's Masterpiece'.

Queen Mary at Southampton.

Queen Mary being berthed.

THE HOOVER IN USE IN BEDROOM OF A SUITE
(R.M.S. QUEEN MARY)

Above: A First Class bedroom is cleaned. Just one of the many advertising postcards issued by companies wanting to associate themselves with the Cunard Queen.

Above right: Carved and pierced screen in limewood by James Woodford.

Right: A detail of the artwork in the First Class Children's Playroom of *Queen Mary.*

Even before the maiden voyage of the *Queen Mary*, much work had already been done on preliminary designs for her sister ship. With a guarantee of funding from the government for construction, plans were well under way on the design. The new, as yet unnamed, ship was to complement the *Queen Mary* and had to be capable of maintaining the same speed as her in moderate weather, i.e. 28.5 knots. Between the two ships, a weekly service had to be maintained across the Atlantic. While much of the design was similar to the *Queen Mary*, almost a decade of progress and the experience of operating the *Mary* led to some radical changes for her sister. First of all, the new liner was to have only twelve boilers instead of the twenty-four of her sister. A direct consequence of this was that the new ship had two funnels instead of the three on the *Queen Mary*. The two funnels themselves were internally braced rather than having the external stays and supports of the *Mary*. This allowed her to have more deck space *à la Normandie*. Another major change would be to transfer the working alleyway from the port side to starboard. This alleyway was the main lifeline of the ship, where the crew could move from one end to the other without being visible and where goods could be transported to different areas of the ship without being visible to the passengers.

After the initial assessment of need, a member of the Naval Architect's department was despatched on a fact-finding mission to visit the *Queen Mary*'s biggest rival – *Normandie*. The French Line's *Normandie* was not just innovative but she was ahead of her time. More ideas and suggestions were utilised from the trip on the *Normandie* than from anywhere else. The gentleman from Cunard disguised himself as a grocer, but became self-conscious when he realised that his disguise may disintegrate after he started to ask technical questions about the ship's performance. How many grocers would want to know technical details about ship design? One of the major changes in the design of the new

ship acquired from the trip on the *Normandie* was more deck space. The new ship also had no well deck.

Two months after the *Queen Mary* had gone into service, the government was approached by Cunard who asked for the use of monies set aside for the second liner, as per the North Atlantic Shipping Act. On 28 July 1936 final confirmation arrived that the government had agreed to the proposals and that the order for the new liner was to be placed with John Brown – builders of the *Queen Mary* and the only shipbuilders in the UK with experience of 80,000-ton liners. It was announced on 30 July 1936 that the new ship would be launched in 1938 and ready for service in 1940. The first passengers booked their places on the maiden voyage – even before the keel had been laid in August 1936! The building contract for the new liner was signed on 1 October 1936 and five days later Cunard signed it – work began on the new liner almost immediately.

Hull 552 made history before her keel was laid. Lloyd's of London and other marine insurance companies insured her hull for £3,760,000, at the time the largest amount insured by private companies for any ship's hull in the world.

The keel laying was on 4 December 1936 and, unlike the *Queen Mary*, there was no ceremony or fuss. By 30 January 1937, the entire keel had been laid in the same builder's berth that had held the *Queen*

Mary for four long years. Like the *Queen Mary* herself, Hull 552 began to take shape, using components from all over the country. Machinery came from Glasgow, Manchester and Tyneside and other parts came from Walsall, Basingstoke, Kilmarnock and Derby. Hull 552 was the product of a whole nation and was responsible directly and indirectly for employing over 50,000 people at any one time for almost two years.

As construction raced ahead, storm clouds were gathering over Europe. Hitler and his Nazi regime were threatening peace, and war seemed inevitable. Slowly, but surely, Hitler and his henchmen began to bully and invade the countries surrounding Germany.

The launch of the *Queen Elizabeth* was set for late September 1938. Again, the current queen was to name the ship. Queen Elizabeth was accompanied by the princesses Elizabeth and Margaret Rose to Clydebank. Unfortunately King George VI cancelled his attendance at the launch as the prime minister needed him for more urgent business in London. The Munich crisis was unfolding and the king and prime minister were heavily involved in averting war in Europe.

The royal party arrived at John Brown's on 27 September 1938 – four years and one day after the launch of the *Queen Elizabeth*'s sister ship, *Queen Mary*. The queen was asked to press the launching button and the royal party waited for the highest point in the tide when it would be safe for the ship to enter the water. In order to alleviate the boredom while waiting for high tide, Lord Aberconway and other officials showed the two royal princesses a working model of the ship on the ways, which illustrated how the new liner would take to the water.

Unfortunately, while doing this, a massive crash of timbers was heard, and the ship started moving prematurely. The queen, remaining quite calm, stepped forward and cut the cord for the wine bottle, naming the ship as she began her first short journey down the slipway to meet her natural element.

Telegraphic Address: "Shipyard" Clydebank."

JOHN BROWN & COMPANY, LIMITED.

Registered Office:
ATLAS WORKS,
SHEFFIELD.
ALDWARKE MAIN,
AND ROTHERHAM MAIN COLLIERIES,
ROTHERHAM.
LONDON OFFICE,
8 THE SANCTUARY, WESTMINSTER.

JWB/AL

Clydebank Engineering & Shipbuilding Works.

Clydebank. 26th April, 1939.

The Secretary,
   Cunard White Star Ltd.,
      Cunard Building,
         LIVERPOOL, 3.

X 17 MAY 1939 X

Dear Sir,

S.S. "QUEEN ELIZABETH"

   We beg to acknowledge receipt of your letter
of the 25th instant enclosing Banker's Order on London
for £25,000, being payment in respect of expenditure
on the above vessel as per Joint Certificate dated 22nd
April, 1939, and we are much obliged for this remittance.

The keel and lower decks of the *Queen Elizabeth* begin to take shape.

Welding and riveting went on almost round the clock.

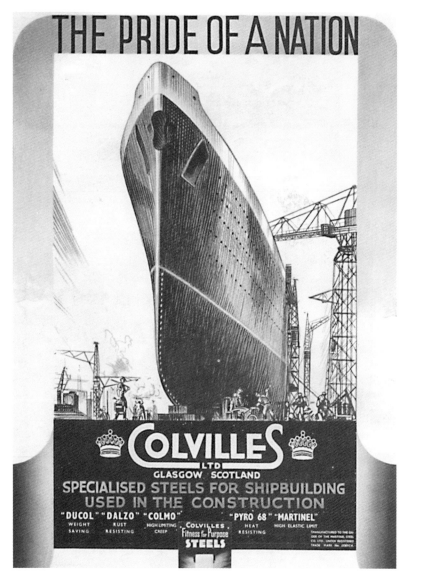

THE PRIDE OF A NATION

COLVILLES
LTD
GLASGOW SCOTLAND
SPECIALISED STEELS FOR SHIPBUILDING
USED IN THE CONSTRUCTION
"DUCOL" "DALZO" "COLMO"   "PYRO 68" "MARTINEL"
WEIGHT   RUST   HIGH LIMITING   HEAT   HIGH ELASTIC LIMIT
SAVING   RESISTING   CREEP   RESISTING
COLVILLES
Fitness for Purpose
STEELS

Queen Elizabeth begins to take shape and is here almost ready for launching.

To have the right angle for launching, the bow was supported on a platform some 20ft in the air.

Work goes on the hull of 552, in summer 1938. Soon the wooden props will be knocked away and she'll be prepared for launching.

After her launch, the great liner, now known as *Queen Elizabeth*, was dragged into the fitting-out basin ready for some of the heavy machinery to be installed and for work to begin on her interiors. Work on the new Cunarder carried on as usual, but the shipyard talk, as it was elsewhere in the country, was that another world war was just about to start.

The political situation in Europe was getting worse and every act of aggression on the part of the Germans brought war closer. People throughout Britain and Europe were frightened at the possibility of another war and many were leaving for safer shores as soon as they could. This was especially true of those Germans and other nationals persecuted by the

Queen Elizabeth hits the water, sending a wave across to the opposite bank of the Clyde and part way up the River Cart.

Nazi government. The *Queen Mary* left Southampton on 30 August 1939, bound for America, with a record number of 2,332 passengers on board, all hoping to get home or escape before war was declared. Unknown to many, the political situation was really just about to get much worse. German troops were already massing on the border with Poland, poised to invade.

As one Queen left Britain, the other remained in the fitting-out basin, her engines and boilers had been installed, and work continued on her interiors. Plumbing, wiring, decorative features and much ancillary equipment still had to be fitted. The *Queen Elizabeth* was a floating building site and would be this way for a few months more. Her maiden

CUNARD WHITE STAR LIMITED AND
JOHN BROWN & COMPANY. LIMITED

STEAMER &
LAUNCHING
PLATFORM

LAUNCH OF S.S. No. 552

from Clydebank Shipyard
on Tuesday, 27th September, 1938,
at 3.15 p.m.

This Card entitles ONE PERSON to go on board the Turbine Steamer
"DUCHESS OF HAMILTON," at Bridge Wharf (South Side), Glasgow.
The Steamer will leave for Clydebank Shipyard at 1.30 p.m.

The Card should be shewn on entering Launching Platform and at the
gangway on returning to Steamer after the Launch.

The Turbine Steamer "DUCHESS OF HAMILTON" will leave Shipyard,
West Side of Dock at 4.15 p.m., and Tea will be served on the return journey.

DRESS: MORNING DRESS   NOT TRANSFERABLE

Provision will be made for parking a limited
number of cars near Bridge Wharf.
Tram Cars, and Buses for Bridge Wharf proceed
down Hope Street and Oswald Street.

Top and right: Ticket and invitation to the launch. These are from the Lobnitz family, who
owned a shipyard in Renfrew. The lucky few travelled downriver from Glasgow on the
Caledonian Steam Packet Co.'s *Duchess of Hamilton.*

The Chairman
and Directors of
Cunard White Star Limited
and of
John Brown and Company
Limited
request the honour of the company of
Lady Lobnitz & Miss Lobnitz
at the Launch, at Clydebank, of
Q.S.T.S. "Queen Elizabeth"
in the presence of
Their Majesties
The King and Queen
on Tuesday, September 27th, at 3.30 p.m.

Her Majesty the Queen
has graciously consented
to perform the naming ceremony.

Clydebank,
August, 1938.

An early reply is requested to
John Brown and Company Limited.
Clydebank.

R.M.S. "QUEEN ELIZABETH" AFTER LAUNCHING 27.9.38.

Above left: Queen Elizabeth on her launch day with an expectant crowd watching from the south bank of the Clyde.

Above: Queen Elizabeth in the water.

26th September, 1938.

The following official statement was issued from Buckingham Palace:—

> *"At the request of the Prime Minister the King has cancelled his journey to Clydebank to-night. The Queen, accompanied by Princess Elizabeth and Princess Margaret, will carry out the programme as arranged. . . ."*

The King graciously sent a message by Her Majesty the Queen. The full text of the Queen's speech appears overleaf.

R.M.S. "QUEEN ELIZABETH" — *Cunard White Star*

EXHIBITION OF THE R.M.S. "QUEEN ELIZABETH" PIANOS

THE DIRECTORS OF RUSHWORTH & DREAPER HAVE PLEASURE IN INVITING YOU TO A SPECIAL PRE-VIEW OF THESE EXQUISITE PIANOFORTES, PRIOR TO THEIR INSTALLATION, IN EARLY FEBRUARY. DESIGNED AND EXECUTED BY THE WORLD'S FOREMOST CRAFTSMEN AND SUPPLIED BY RUSHWORTH & DREAPER, THEY ARE A WORTHY CONTRIBUTION TO THE SPLENDOUR OF BRITAIN'S LATEST MARITIME MASTERPIECE

To be held in the Music Room, Rushworth and Dreaper's Building, 13 Islington, Liverpool, 3

Commencing Monday, 29th JANUARY, 1940, Daily 9 a.m. to 6 p.m.

[P.T.O.

Top right: Just a small part of one of the two huge engine rooms.

Left: A programme for the Exhibition of Pianos in January 1940. This programme was issued before war started in September 1939.

passenger-carrying voyage was to be in April 1940 and plans were being made despite the increasingly bad political climate in Europe.

On 1 September 1939 Poland was invaded. Two days later Britain and France honoured their agreements with the Poles to come to their aid and declared war on Nazi Germany.

The bow of 552 rises into the Clydebank sky. An idea of the scale can be gathered by looking at the men at her bow.

On 3 September 1939, the *Queen Mary* steamed into New York harbour with her record 2,332 passengers, all hoping to get to America before war started. As the *Mary* drew into her berth at Pier 90, another victim of the war in Europe – the *Normandie* – also lay at her berth, having arrived a few days earlier crowded with refugees and Americans returning from Europe. For both ships the immediate future was uncertain – neither could go back home for fear of attack by submarine or German aeroplanes.

Meanwhile, on the other side of the Atlantic, the *Queen Elizabeth* was also causing logistical problems. In her fitting-out berth at John Brown's shipyard the *Queen Elizabeth* was a sitting duck. The Germans knew that bombing such a massive ship *in situ* would bring havoc to Britain's shipbuilding industry and it would effectively close John Brown's down for the duration. The number of men involved in salvage would be huge, and a wrecked hull would remove valuable skills from the war effort. Refitting of the hull would also block one of the biggest fitting-out berths in the country. If the *Queen Elizabeth* was completed, then she could be converted into a troop carrier or used for some other naval purpose. Another aspect was morale. If the giant liner was bombed, it would be a fantastic coup for the Germans and British morale would be extremely low – especially as the ship was named after the British consort.

The Admiralty was concerned that the new Cunarder was in the fitting-out berth. The battleship HMS *Duke of York* was due to be launched and the *Queen Elizabeth* was in the basin that the *Duke of York* would be fitted out in after her launch. No other warships could be refitted while the *Elizabeth* was still there. This meant that vital repairs and refitting of warships were being delayed. Added to this was the threat of destruction by German bombers. In fact, Clydebank was blitzed in 1941 and much of the town destroyed. The *Queen Elizabeth* had to move!

Opposite: Two views of *Queen Elizabeth* travelling down the Clyde and to safety in New York, March 1940.

Above and above right: Steaming across 3,000 miles of U-boat-infested waters, *Queen Elizabeth* approaches America and safety.

Right: A triumphant maiden voyage sees *Queen Elizabeth* arrive at New York, untested but safe.

For the ship herself, life had changed. The king and queen were due to have toured her engine rooms and third-class accommodation on 23 August 1939, but this visit was shelved due to the political crisis. Her maiden voyage, set for 24 April 1940, was cancelled when war was declared. Then, starting on 4 September 1939, she was unceremoniously painted grey from bow to stern.

The anxiety the new Cunarder caused to both Cunard and the British Admiralty was enormous. Meetings were held to decide what to do with her. One suggestion was that she be moved to the Gareloch and moored there, another was for her to be moved to Southampton. The idea of sending her to a neutral port, such as New York, was rejected as her engines and equipment had not been tested. By the end of September 1939, work had stopped on Hull 552 because men were needed for the vital task of refitting naval ships. For a while *Queen Elizabeth* became a ghost ship, abandoned by all but essential care and maintenance workers.

On 2 November 1939 the Ministry of Shipping granted a special licence to John Brown's to resume the fitting-out work on Hull 552 to cover essential electrical and plumbing work only. By the end of December her engines were turning by steam for the very first time and tests were made of the emergency equipment fitted to the main engines. Then, early in February 1940, Cunard received a letter from Winston Churchill, ordering that the ship be moved from Britain as soon as possible and for her to remain as long as the order was in force.

In theory, this order was understandable, but it was a little harder to put into practice. Firstly, there were only a few ports that could take a vessel of this size, and then there were problems with the tides on the Clyde. On only two days per year was there guaranteed to be enough depth of water in the upper river to ensure a safe passage downriver for the *Queen*. On each of these two days there were two suitable tides that reached the optimum height. The first possible day that the tides were

suitable was at the end of February 1940. It was planned that the giant Cunarder would be floated out on the first tide and the battleship *Duke of York* launched and brought into the fitting-out basin on the second tide. If these two operations could not be completed on that tide, then it was another six months before the task could be attempted again.

As work had resumed on the new Cunarder, rumours and speculation began to grow as to what her fate was. The British government, being wary of potential German spies operating in Britain, was extremely careful not to give anything away as to the fate of the ship. A deliberate false rumour was circulated prior to her setting sail that she was going to Southampton to be dry-docked. The King George V dry dock was the only one big enough to accept her in the United Kingdom. The government made the rumour extremely convincing, the graving dock was prepared, 500 crew were signed on for a short coastal voyage, the Southampton Pilot went aboard in the Clyde to take her to her new home, and crates of furniture and supplies were sent to Southampton in preparation for her arrival. Hotel rooms were booked and she was registered at Customs House – her official number being 166290, signal GBSS. So convincing were these rumours that, on the day she was supposed to arrive in Southampton, German bombers were hovering around Southampton Docks waiting to bomb their latest victim!

A crew for the new ship was assembled and the *Queen Elizabeth* left her fitting-out basin on 26 February 1940, escorted by six tugs. Unlike her sister ship, the *Queen Mary*, there was no cheering or publicity. A few people gathered along the banks of the Clyde as she made her slow journey down the upper reaches of the Clyde. A ship as large as this, moving down the Clyde, would attract attention; it was unavoidable. But few watched her go initially. By the time she was part way down the Clyde thousands were watching her make her slow progress downriver. Work stopped at other shipyards as she passed while RAF fighter planes circled overhead to make sure no German bombers could get near. After five hours sailing, she finally reached the Tail of the Bank in the early evening. She had almost grounded in the same spot as her sister at Rashilee Light, when her stern was caught by the tide and her bow became embedded on the bank. Fortunately, the tugs managed to pull her off (although this took almost an hour) and she continued on her way. She anchored at the Tail of the Bank near Gourock for a couple of days while trials were made to test her engines and steering gear and to adjust her compasses. Then she was officially handed over to Cunard White Star.

On 2 March 1940 a King's Messenger arrived on board with a special sealed envelope. This contained the Captain's orders and he was under strict instructions that they were not to be opened until the liner was at sea. The crew were assembled and given the option of leaving the ship now or staying for the journey. Only a few crew members left and they were kept isolated until the ship was well on her way to her final destination.

R.M.S. Queen Elizabeth

MAIDEN VOYAGE

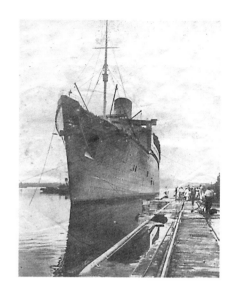

Above: Queen Elizabeth tendered by landing craft at an unknown location.

Top right: Queen Elizabeth went from New York to Singapore, where she entered dry dock for the first time to have her hull cleaned and painted.

THE VOYAGE

The *Queen Elizabeth*, under the watchful eye of Captain Townley, departed from the Clyde on 2 March 1940, accompanied by four destroyers as far as Rathlin Island. Her orders now were to head out to sea at speed. There, Captain Townley opened up the sealed envelope given to him by the King's Messenger. The orders were to head for New York.

This was a perilous undertaking for an untried ship: no one knew whether her brand-new engines would carry her across the Atlantic. She was unarmed and unescorted. Her only protection was her speed. Conditions on board were very basic. No major fitting out had been done prior to her leaving Clydebank and there were wires dangling from the ceilings of the cabins and public rooms. There was little in the way of heating and in February, on the North Atlantic, this was a major problem. Inside the ship, the eerie silence was punctuated occasionally by echoes caused by the lack of carpets, furniture or fittings. At night blackout conditions were observed, so on deck everything was pitch black. Daily inspections of equipment were made and adjustments were carried out as necessary.

To relieve boredom, crew members formed the 'Unruffled Elizabethans' Club'. The club was for those 'on the combined trial trip and maiden voyage of HMS *Queen Elizabeth*, leaving Glasgow for New York on 26 February 1940. On account of wartime conditions the plaudits of the public were replaced by the providential mist and an escort of HM destroyers and seaplanes.' The aim of the club was 'to establish the proposition that true Twentieth Century Elizabethans are able to remain under all conditions completely unruffled!' Club members amused themselves on board by giving musical recitals and telling stories – anything to relieve the boredom!

THE ARRIVAL

After a few days of speculation a mystery ship assumed to be the *Queen Elizabeth* was first spotted approaching the coast at high speed by a plane off Fire Island, near New York, on 7 March 1940. The crew of the plane at first couldn't recognise this speeding giant as no one on this side of the Atlantic had seen the *Queen Elizabeth* before and no one in America was expecting her. Only the offices of Cunard White Star knew of the imminent arrival and that was because they had been approached by a Special Agent just prior to the *Queen Elizabeth*'s arrival to inform them she was on her way.

She anchored off 'quarantine', waited for high tide, then made her way up the Hudson River. As news circulated around New York of this extraordinary event, crowds gathered to see this new superliner's maiden arrival. *Queen Elizabeth* gracefully pulled into dock and met, for the first time, her sister ship *Queen Mary*, and also her greatest rival *Normandie*, which was berthed alongside them. When the *Elizabeth* was safely docked, the area around her remained sealed off for fear that German agents may get on board and try to sabotage her. Only official visitors were allowed up the gangway.

The crew, with many workmen from John Brown's shipyard, were taken home on board the Cunard intermediate steamer *Scythia* and, while in New York, the *Elizabeth* had her electrical and plumbing works installed, her heating system put into working order and life-saving equipment added. In New York, she had a small maintenance staff and a single boiler was kept in steam – just enough to keep her ticking over and to provide power and heat for essential needs.

It was decided in March 1940 that the *Queen Mary* should be converted to a troop carrier. On 21 March, she sailed down the Hudson, on her way to Australia, to be fitted out. In September 1940 a meeting between the Ministry of Shipping and Cunard took place. It was decided

The three greatest liners of all time together for the first, and last, time.

During her time in Singapore, the *Elizabeth*'s engines were overhauled, the hull scraped for the first time, guns fitted and she was repainted. After leaving Singapore, she headed for Sydney, where the Cockatoo Docks & Engineering Co. began her full conversion to a troopship. During this time they also erected hospital compartments in the main lounge and smoking room, and a special isolation unit in the stern. The Turkish Baths were converted to an X-ray department.

In April 1941, the two mighty Queens met for the first time as troopships. They sailed on a trooping run from Australia to Suez, accompanied by the *Mauretania*. The main areas of concern were the heat – which, on a transatlantic liner not designed for hot climates, was oppressive – and the threat from German submarines and commerce raiders that may be operating in the Pacific and Indian oceans. *Elizabeth* made three trooping voyages, each lasting six weeks. She ferried Australian troops to Suez and prisoners of war back to Australia.

In 1942 Australia came under threat from a new enemy – Japan. In December 1941, the Japanese had attacked the US naval base at Pearl Harbor, as well as Malaya and Hong Kong. These acts turned the conflict from a European and African war to a truly worldwide one. Japanese advances in South East Asia and the Pacific were swift, and soon Australia itself was under threat. Many troops had gone to fight in Africa and the need for reinforcements was desperate. As a result, the *Elizabeth* was sent to bring American troops to Australia. She headed to Esquimalt, British Columbia, for dry-docking before carrying on to San Francisco to embark troops. Esquimalt was one of the few large dry docks still available to the Allies, as Singapore and its dry dock were under threat and were to be lost in February 1942 after the fall of the colony to the Japanese. The *Elizabeth*'s arrival at Esquimalt was a slight farce as she missed the high tide – in order to get the depth of water to

that the war was obviously going to continue for a long time and that the *Elizabeth* would follow the *Mary* and become a troop carrier. October 1940 saw the *Scythia* and *Samaria* bring a crew across from Britain for the *Elizabeth* and she sailed down the Hudson in November 1940 with a crew of 465 on board. This new adventure took the *Elizabeth* via Trinidad – where she was replenished with fuel and fresh water – then on to Cape Town and finally to Singapore. The *Elizabeth* received an extremely cool welcome there, mainly because, during the *Queen Mary*'s time in Singapore, some members of the crew had become rowdy and demolished a pub during a brawl. The *Elizabeth*'s crew had been warned that this type of behaviour would not be tolerated, and that the privileges that had initially been given to the *Queen Mary*'s crew had been withdrawn.

een Mary - World's largest ship - at Cape Town.

dry-dock safely – and had to go on a cruise to nowhere until the next high tide. The dry dock was damaged by the anti-submarine devices on her bow as she entered it.

After refitting in Esquimalt, she headed for San Francisco, where she loaded thousands of American troops bound for Australia. In San Francisco she ran aground but luckily tugs pulled her off. She sailed on 19 March 1942 laden with 8,000 troops and a crew of 875. After this trooping voyage she was ordered to return to New York to be used to transport troops across the Atlantic.

TRANSATLANTIC TROOPERS

Queen Elizabeth met her sister for the third time at Sydney on 6 April 1942. *Queen Mary* was outbound to New York having deposited over 8,000 troops at Sydney while the *Elizabeth* was inbound with her contingent of reinforcements. She left Sydney that same month with a

Above left: Queen Mary is bunkered on the Clyde.

Left: Queen Mary at Cape Town on one of her voyages to Australia and Singapore. This view probably dates from 1940.

few civilian passengers to return to New York via Cape Town and Rio. She arrived there in late May 1942.

It had been realised that to even contemplate attacking the Germans on mainland Europe would need hundreds of thousands of men and millions of tons of equipment. The only ships capable of carrying the huge quantities of men safely and speedily across the 3,000 miles of U-boat-infested water were ocean liners, used to travelling at high speed. The Queens *Mary* and *Elizabeth* soon became the major transportation method for moving the huge volumes of troops required across the Atlantic. The carrying capacity of each ship was continually being increased until each ship could carry a whole division of troops at a time. The most carried on any journey by the Queens was about 16,000. The *Queen Elizabeth* made three trips between Halifax and Gourock, and thirty-one trips between New York and Gourock.

Boarding a whole division was a major operation. Prior to sailing, a major conference was held with each division to find out about the journey and the details of the ship; then Advance Teams of about 2,000 to 2,500 men were sent aboard the ship for familiarisation. At Camp Kilmer 'mock-ups' of the Queens were built and the other soldiers (not in Advance Teams) were trained in boarding speedily and given the

Above: The degaussing cable used to keep the ship safe in the vicinity of magnetic mines is clearly shown in this mid-war shot.

Compliments of the Season

DINNER

Tomato Soup

Halibut, Hollandaise Sauce

Braised Ham, Madere

Roast Turkey, Stuffing, Cranberry Sauce

Fresh Broccoli Green Peas

Boiled and Roast Potatoes

Cold : Roast Beef Roast Lamb

Combination Salad

Cream and Russian Dressings

Plum Pudding Mince Pies

Ice Cream

Fresh Fruit Coffee

R.M.S "Queen Elizabeth" CHRISTMAS DAY, 1945

Above: Homecoming troops arrive safely in New York in 1945.

Above right: The stern of *Queen Elizabeth* is repainted in Cunard colours.

Right: HMS *Vanguard* at the Tail of the Bank with *Queen Elizabeth* being repainted in the background.

Above: Fully refurbished, *Queen Elizabeth* has steam up and is prepared to go on her official sea trials with HM Queen Elizabeth on board. Soon she will leave on her first passenger voyage from Southampton to New York.

plans of their particular sections of the two ships. The soldiers were also instructed in such subjects as blackouts, emergency drills and procedures of abandoning ship.

On the way to Scotland, the troops had to put all the knowledge they had gleamed at Camp Kilmer into use. They learned about colour-coded areas – no soldier was to stray outside his allotted area except for food, as overloading of personnel in a particular area could prove hazardous to the ship. All soldiers were required to carry their life jackets with them at all times and strict penalties awaited any soldier who did not have his

life jacket on his person. Soldiers were fed twice a day. While on board they were given lectures on how to behave towards British people and the differences in culture. While on their trooping voyages, the Queens carried American soldiers to Scotland and on the return voyages they were transformed into floating hospitals, carrying home many casualties and also taking prisoners of war to internment in the USA and Canada. Gourock was chosen as the British port of call because Southampton was too close to the front, Liverpool was used for cargo and Gourock itself had deep water close to shore and more than enough space for the

Queens. Here the Queens anchored offshore and everyone was taken off by tender. These were mainly ex-Clyde pleasure steamers which looked like tiny rowing boats in comparison to the 1,000-ft-long Queens.

For their safety, while crossing the Atlantic, the two ships kept to a pattern of zigzagging, which, combined with their great speed, meant that they could outmanoeuvre any U-boat which crossed their path. Before the U-boat could target on a Queen, she was gone! The two ships were also armed, but the guns were never fired in anger, as the ships were too fast for any U-boat and they were never sighted by enemy aircraft.

REPATRIATION

In May 1945 the Germans surrendered and the troops were anxious to return home. After discussions between American and British governments, it was decided that the *Queen Mary* should be used to repatriate American soldiers and the *Queen Elizabeth* and *Aquitania* used for British and Commonwealth troops.

On 20 August 1945 the *Queen Elizabeth* sailed up the Solent to Southampton for the first time. In the Main Lounge of the *Elizabeth* the Mayor and Mayoress of Southampton gave a toast to the Captain and crew for 'bringing Southampton's baby home safely'. Then repatriation voyages began. From August to October the *Queen Elizabeth* carried American troops and on 22 October 1945 the first Canadian troops were taken home. The ship travelled to Halifax where the Canadians gave them a huge welcome. Captain Bisset, Commodore of the Cunard Line, had his reservations about making Halifax trips a regular occurrence, especially in winter. The dock at Halifax was a wharf and wasn't enclosed, meaning that if a south-easterly gale hit the ship she might break free from her moorings and cause untold damage to herself and the dock. Other Cunard captains considered his opinion correct,

but the Canadian government protested vehemently. The final decision lay with the owners of the ship, who agreed with Bisset. The Canadian government had to accept Cunard's decision that all future Canadian trooping voyages would end in New York during the winter months.

After these trooping voyages, the *Elizabeth* was converted into a giant floating nursery, to take Canadian war brides and their children to their new homeland.

THE CAPTAIN SLEEPS WITH THE MAGNA CARTA

On a return voyage from New York in January 1946, the *Queen Elizabeth* sailed into Southampton with the Lincoln copy of the Magna Carta. The document had originally been taken on board the *Queen Mary* to be exhibited at the New York World's Fair in 1939. When war was declared, the Magna Carta was then transferred from New York to the Library of Congress. When Pearl Harbor was bombed, it was moved to a vault in Fort Knox. On the Magna Carta's return journey to Britain, Commodore Bisset received it from the British Consul-General in New York and it was to be placed in the ship's strongroom, but it was too large. The safest place on the ship after this was under the Commodore's bed! There it remained until it safely reached Southampton.

When the *Queen Elizabeth* arrived back in Southampton on 6 March 1946 after her last wartime sailing, the crew were given a holiday for three weeks and only a few crew were left on board to maintain her. Unfortunately, just two days after, a fire broke out among some medical equipment and highly flammable materials, which had been stored in a compartment on the Promenade Deck. The *Queen*'s own fire crew had been released from their duties just prior to this and Southampton's own fire brigade had to be called in. It took fire crews three hours to get the blaze under control. Lifeboats had to be lowered with firemen in them as the fire brigade's ladders could not reach the Promenade Deck. The ship suffered some flooding and warped steel beams.

REFITTING AFTER THE WAR

After a few weeks in Southampton, the *Queen Elizabeth* sailed to the Clyde for refitting. She was too large to go back up the Clyde to John Brown's, so John Brown's had to come to her. The workers commuted from Clydebank to Gourock, then were shuttled back and forth to the great liner just offshore by an array of small boats. During this time her war equipment was removed, her portholes scraped clean of blackout paint, and her galleys and electrical equipment renewed. More than 2,000 workers were involved in the task. After the fire in Southampton, a Fire Security Brigade was permanently kept on board to observe the correct use of acetylene torches and electrical welding equipment.

The *Queen Elizabeth* returned to Southampton for the final phase of the conversion on 16 June 1946. On 6 August she entered the King George V Graving Dock for inspections and refit of her underwater sections. More than 1,000 workers from John Brown's travelled to Southampton to finish internal renovations and refitting work and they were housed in Nissen huts located at Chandlersford, near Southampton, and bussed to the liner on a daily basis.

Co-ordinating the return of furniture to the massive liner was a nightmare as fixtures and furnishings were stored all over the world. Some of her furniture had been taken out at New York, some stored in California and other bits and pieces in Australia. Hangers were rented at Eastleigh airport in order to receive the fixtures and fittings as they arrived from storage.

Although not quite as popular as the *Queen Mary*, the new Cunarder captured the imagination of the British people. It was felt that in these

Princess Elizabeth times the ship on one of her speed trials.

bleak and desolate post-war times, the ship gave people something to be proud of. She was a symbol of what Britain and British people could achieve, even in wartime – she represented a 'new British Age'. It was also acknowledged that Britain had the largest ship in the world, *Queen Elizabeth*, as well as the fastest, *Queen Mary*. Both ships were a source of immense pride. The government was careful, however, to let the British people know that these ships were renovated without the use of public funds. After six years of war, it was felt that the British people would not take too kindly to the government being frivolous, especially considering the rebuilding needed in Britain's houses and industries. Special press releases were issued to reinforce the message and to avoid any problems with the refits of both ships.

As the time of her first post-war commercial sailing approached, the press were invited on board the *Queen Elizabeth* during August and September 1946. Although very opulent and grand, opinions were divided on the new Cunarder. The *Elizabeth* was more modern than the *Queen Mary* but this did not suit everyone's tastes. She was a mixture of late 1930s and mid-1940s styling. Cunard was very coy about letting the public know just what the original interiors of the ship had been like. Fittings and furnishings must have changed in the six and a half years since her first sailing. New public areas were also added to the *Queen Elizabeth* (such as the Garden Room and the Cinema). No one but the management at Cunard knew what the ship was to have been like originally. As a result of the years between conception and maiden voyage and the need to reuse many pre-war fittings, while mixing these with post-war items as necessary, her design was less coherent than the very art deco *Queen Mary*. It was to be a problem that dogged her all her life. The *Queen Mary* had been designed as a whole at one time and the *Elizabeth* just hadn't. This perhaps explains why she was always less popular than her older sister.

HM Queen Elizabeth steers the ship under the watchful eye of a Cunard Quartermaster.

SEA TRIALS

At the start of October 1946, over six years after the *Elizabeth* had been due to perform her original sea trials, she headed off from Southampton back to the Clyde. On 7 October she completed two unofficial sprints of over 30 knots. These were witnessed by the Chairmen of Cunard and John Brown's, as well as officials from the Ministry of Transport.

The *Elizabeth* had some very important visitors on 8 October. Queen Elizabeth herself, accompanied by princesses Elizabeth and Margaret

Rose, sailed out on the Clyde pleasure steamer *Queen Mary II* for a tour of her namesake. The princesses were given a stopwatch each while on the Bridge to measure the 'trialled run' over the measured mile, of which there were two on the Clyde. After this Queen Elizabeth took the wheel and steered the largest ship in the world down the Firth of Clyde.

A PASSENGER SHIP AT LAST

The *Elizabeth* sailed from Gourock to Southampton on 9 October 1946 with 400 VIP passengers. The passenger list read like a veritable who's who. Among the passengers were directors of Cunard and its associated companies, shipyard owners, shipping line owners, and many other dignitaries. On a ship supposed to hold over 2,000 passengers, 400 people rattled around. Entertainment was laid on and they were asked to test Cunard's famed service and quality to the full, providing comments and constructive criticism. Included in the programme of events were tours of the public and passenger accommodation as well as the kitchens and storerooms. Other entertainment included films, dancing, horse racing and deck games.

On 13 October 1946 the ship arrived at Southampton to begin her commercial service.

Above left: The interior of a boiler room.

Above right: The Bridge.

Left: Their Majesties had a full inspection of the ship and visited all parts including the engine and boiler rooms.

The Chairman and Directors of
Cunard White Star Limited
request the pleasure of the company of

_____

on board their
R.M.S. "Queen Elizabeth"
for a trip
from the Clyde to Southampton
embarking at Gourock 6·30 p.m.
on Wednesday, 9th October, 1946,
disembarking at Southampton on the
morning of Friday 11th October, 1946.

September, 1946.

CUNARD WHITE STAR LIMITED.

———

R.M.S. "QUEEN ELIZABETH"
CLYDE TO SOUTHAMPTON

———

Embarking by tender from Gourock Pier
6-30 p.m., Wednesday, 9th October, 1946

Name of Guest(s) ..... *Miss M. Lidbury* ....

Room Number .... M. 34 ....

...1... Ticket(s) enclosed for travel by special train from Euston 9-10 a.m. 9th October.

PLEASE PRESENT THIS CARD ON EMBARKATION AT TENDER.

R.M.S. " QUEEN ELIZABETH "

Wednesday, October 9th, 1946.

————

    Due to lack of sufficient time there may be a number of details in the staterooms where further attention is necessary or additional fitments required.   For example certain small mirrors have been mislaid on the railway.   These have been recovered and will be fitted in a few days.

    All the rooms are being examined, but in the meantime the Company would be very grateful for a note from their guests calling attention to such features so that these can be dealt with as early as possible.

ITINERARY

————

9TH OCTOBER, 1946

GREENOCK	Depart	8.00 pm
LITTLE CUMBRAE	Estimated to pass at	9.00 pm
AILSA CRAIG	,,	10.10 pm

10TH OCTOBER, 1946

CALF OF MAN	,,	1.25 am
SMALLS	,,	7.20 am
LONGSHIPS	,,	11.31 am
LIZARD HEAD	,,	12.44 pm
EDDYSTONE	,,	2.21 pm
START POINT	,,	3.21 pm
PORTLAND BILL	,,	5.22 pm
ST. CATHERINE POINT	,,	7.11 pm
NAB TOWER	,,	7.51 pm
SOUTHAMPTON	Arrive	10.30 pm

Distance approximately 595 miles

CUNARD
WHITE STAR

CHAPTER FIVE

GRACIOUS LIVING AT ITS BEST

MAIDEN VOYAGE

The *Queen Elizabeth* sailed on her post-war maiden voyage on Wednesday 16 October 1946. On board for the momentous occasion were 2,288 passengers, a few of whom had reserved cabins for the first maiden voyage in April 1940 and, with eternal optimism, had still retained their bookings.

As with the *Queen Mary* ten years before, the passenger list read like a who's who of the great and good. On board were cabinet ministers, businessmen, peers, film stars and a US Senator. There were also eighty journalists on board, recording the voyage for posterity.

Although the meals on board were not as glamorous as those on the pre-war *Queen Mary* voyages, many of the passengers had not had as much quality food in years. Rationing was still in force in Britain and much of the food for the maiden voyage had been imported especially from Canada and the USA on board the *Aquitania*. On finding that quality food in quantity was freely available on board, many people ate more than their digestive systems could cope with and ended up at the ship's hospital with a variety of complaints.

For those capable of surviving the rich food, five days of life on board became one huge party with music and dancing, film shows, horse racing, deck games and swimming. More radio messages were received and sent from the ship – 66,306 words – than on the maiden voyage of the *Queen Mary*. The shops on board also did a roaring trade as goods were available that couldn't be bought in Britain including clothes which did not need ration coupons. Also available were chocolate, perfume, stockings and other luxuries. Trade was so brisk that the shops had to be locked and only a certain number of customers were allowed in at any one time.

The *Elizabeth* arrived in New York on 21 October 1946. She crossed the Atlantic in 4 days, 16 hours and 18 minutes at an average speed of

Top: Entering King George V Dry Dock after her trip from the Clyde in 1946 to have her hull painted.

Above: Queen Mary and *Queen Elizabeth* meet in Southampton, on 27 September 1946.

29 knots. A possible threat to her triumphant arrival in New York was closely averted. A dock strike could have meant redirecting to Halifax, but as this was her maiden voyage no one had the heart to turn her away. A flotilla of small boats met the giant Queen as she arrived in her Cunard peacetime livery for the first time, and accompanied her into the harbour of New York.

STOWAWAYS

Surprisingly, on the post-war maiden voyage, the *Queen Elizabeth* acquired two stowaways. Checks had been made to ensure that there were no human stowaways on board, but two animal stowaways were discovered. The first was a tagged racing pigeon that landed on the ship in the English Channel. The bird had a free run to New York and back and was dutifully returned to its owner on arrival at Southampton on the return voyage. The second stowaway was a Persian cat. It was believed that the poor creature had sneaked aboard at Southampton and then managed to get itself locked in a cupboard. A couple of days later the door was opened and the starving cat appeared. It later ended up in a passenger's cabin where it was reported to a member of the crew. Later, after the cat had recovered, it was put to work on the ship!

A DREAM ALMOST SEEN THROUGH

The Queens were the dream of one man, Sir Percy Bates, Chairman of Cunard, who had instigated their construction. He watched them progress through design to reality and fought for them every step of the way, even through the most difficult of times.

Sir Percy was due to sail on board the maiden voyage. He had travelled on the coastal cruise with his family, but on the day before the

ABSTRACT OF THE LOG OF THE				Maiden
CUNARD WHITE STAR				Voyage

R.M.S. "QUEEN ELIZABETH"

COMMODORE SIR JAMES BISSET, C.B.E., R.D., R.N.R., LL.D.

NEW YORK TO SOUTHAMPTON

Date (1946)		Dist.	Latitude	Longitude	Weather, etc.
Fri.	Oct. 25		N.	W.	At 5.57 p.m. E.S.T., Left Coy.'s Berth, N.Y.
,,	,, 25				At 8.30 p.m. E.S.T., A.C.L.V abeam (depart.)
Sat.,	,, 26	406	40.39	65.02	Moderate breeze, mod. sea, fine and clear
Sunday,	,, 27	650	41.56	50.47	Fresh winds, rough sea, slight swell, overcast
Monday,	,, 28	660	46.43	37.02	Gentle breeze, slight sea, cloudy and clear
Tuesday,	,, 29	628	49.24	21.56	Mod. winds and sea, slight swell, cloudy, fine
Wed.,	,, 30	607	49.48	6.24	Strong to fresh winds, rough sea, cloudy, fine
,,	,, 30	223	To Nab	Tower	At 22.48 p.m. (G.M.T.) Nab Tower
					abeam (arrival)
	Total	3,174	nautical miles		

PASSAGE - 4 days, 21 hours, 18 minutes   AVERAGE SPEED - 27.06 knots

maiden voyage, he complained of feeling ill and collapsed in his office. Lady Bates cancelled their voyage and Sir Percy died just before his beloved *Queen Elizabeth* left on her first post-war commercial sailing. A memorial service was held on board ship at the same time his funeral took place in England.

THE QUEEN'S SUCCESS

Regular travellers had their favourite ship, often being greeted by cabin stewards and waiters they considered to be old friends, and many of the 'smart-set' who regularly travelled the Atlantic often switched allegiance from the *Queen Mary* to the *Queen Elizabeth* and were equally at home on either. The largest liner in the world became extremely fashionable

The Chairman and Directors
of
Cunard White Star Limited
request the pleasure of the company of

at Luncheon on board their
R. M. S. "Queen Elizabeth"
at Southampton on Saturday, 12th October, 1946.

Cunard Building,
Liverpool, 3.
September, 1946.

because she was the newest ship with the most modern décor. Cunard had the enviable reputation of having the fastest ship – the *Queen Mary* – and the largest ship – the *Queen Elizabeth*.

The interiors of the *Queen Elizabeth* were a blended mixture of 1930s art deco and mid-1940s. The interiors did not please everyone as sometimes the different periods of design failed to blend together very well. Many of the artists commissioned had done work on the *Queen Mary* though and were popular among travellers. Artists who created artwork and designs for both ships included Anna Zinkeisen, Macdonald Gill and Bainbridge Copnall.

VERANDAH GRILL

On the Queens, the Verandah Grill was *the* place to be seen. Many of the rich and famous passengers dined here as a way of escaping the crowds in the main First Class Restaurant. The Grill had an intimate atmosphere, and diners received the best of food and entertainment the ship offered. The Verandah Grill was the only restaurant on the whole ship with a cover charge for meals. It was situated on Sun Deck and the walls were covered with an ivory-coloured sycamore veneer, and an illuminated decorative glass balustrade surrounded the dance floor. Jan Juta designed a decorated glass screen at each corner of the Grill, which was also equipped with a mechanically controlled, colour-changing light system used to alter the lighting according to the music being played.

QUEEN ELIZABETH

October 16, 1946 ushered in a new era in ocean travel

Above and opposite: At Southampton, preparing for her maiden voyage. Southampton had suffered greatly during the war and much of the damage was still to be repaired, as can be seen by the bomb damage still extant on the left view of the Cunard passenger terminal.

The Verandah Grill.

THE FIRST CLASS RESTAURANT

The First Class Restaurant was 110ft long by 115ft wide and was situated on R Deck. It was approached from a high foyer. Above the main entrance to the restaurant was a motif of the carved coat of arms of Her Majesty Queen Elizabeth. The motif was carved from lime-tree wood by Mr Bainbridge Copnall, who had carved fourteen wooden panels for the *Queen Mary* illustrating the history of shipping. Mr Copnall also carved the two figures representing Elizabethan heralds that stood just under the coat of arms.

In the restaurant itself, Copnall was responsible for a variety of sculptures and carvings including a large clock face carved in lime-tree wood that took the form of signs of the zodiac. He also carved two large sculptures at the aft end of the restaurant representing 'The Fisherman'

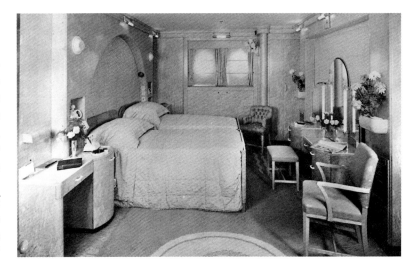

and 'The Huntress'. Between these two figures hung a large tapestry designed by Eleanor Esmonde-White and Leroux Smith Leroux.

A silk replica of the Queen's Standard (given to the ship by the queen on 8 October 1946) hung above the restaurant entrance.

The main walls of the restaurant were covered with London plane tree burr while the centre of the restaurant was raised and the outer parts were divided into three areas. The central area had a canopy at ceiling level and was decorated with gilded ornament.

PRIVATE DINING ROOMS

The Private Dining Rooms were designed for first-class passengers who wanted small, intimate dinner parties. The *Queen Elizabeth* had three altogether with two on the starboard side and one on the port side. The

forward starboard private dining room was panelled with a rare veneer of oyster aspen. The aft private dining room on the starboard side was panelled with English elm burr and the aft port private dining room was panelled with claret-and-white-coloured leather. Two of the private dining rooms had decorative glass panels by Mr Jan Juta.

MAIN LOUNGE

The central portion of the main lounge rose to 23ft in height over two decks and the principal woods used were Canadian maple cluster with finishing of elm burr. This panelling was balanced with panels of leather covered in light grey, pale blue and buff. Here from 1948 there was a painting by Sir Oswald Birley of Her Majesty Queen Elizabeth, which faced the front entrance, and marquetry panels of playing cards, designed by George Ramon, were also incorporated into the design, along with two flower studies by Cedric Morris.

The cabin-class smoking room, with chairs in blue and fawn leather.

THE SALON

The Salon was also known as the Ballroom. The walls of this room were quilted in satin and the room included a glass panel by Jan Juta depicting a jungle scene. There were four recesses on the outer edge of the room lined with ivory sycamore. The Salon was installed with the latest equipment for changing the light according to the type of music being played.

SMOKING ROOM

The Smoking Room was panelled in four distinct veneers of chestnut tree, grown on the Isle of Wight. There were three large carvings by Dennis Dunlop representing Hunting, Fishing and Shooting. On the forward bulkhead in this room was a large clock face by MacDonald Gill. Below the clock face there was a decorative map of Britain and the United States with models representing both RMS *Queen Mary* and RMS *Queen Elizabeth* that moved between the two countries in direct relation to their actual whereabouts. Also in this room were two paintings by the fabulous marine artist Norman Wilkinson.

OBSERVATION LOUNGE AND COCKTAIL BAR

Running the full width of the ship on Promenade Deck, the Observation Lounge was semicircular in shape. Its tables were set in terraces and the floor was sunk below the level of the rest of the room. The outer walls were panelled in sycamore, dyed to the colour of lobster shell. This was inlaid with various panels depicting scenes from the circus, by George Ramon. These panels were decorated using many different kinds of wood. The inner section of the Cocktail Lounge was panelled in silver sycamore inlaid with metal stars.

Above: Garland in main restaurant in the form of the signs of the zodiac by Bainbridge Copnall.

Below: Part of the design of the Canterbury Pilgrims in coloured woods.

Left: Tapestry from the restaurant by Eleanor Esmonde-White and Leroux Smith-Leroux.
Below left: Bas-reliefs by Norman Forest above the fireplace in the cabin-class smoking room.

MAIN HALL

Off the Main Hall was the entrance to the Main Lounge. The walls were covered in two tones of cream leather. At the head of the stairs was a sculpture by Maurice Lambert of 'Orcades'. The opposite wall contained a large marquetry panel by George Ramon depicting Chaucer's Canterbury Pilgrims.

GARDEN LOUNGES

The garden lounge was a new post-war addition to the *Queen Elizabeth* and had not been in the original design. The success of garden lounges (and especially the fantastic Winter Garden) on the *Normandie* had been noted and incorporated into the design of the *Lizzie*. During her refit the *Queen Mary* was also retrofitted with a garden lounge. On the *Queen Elizabeth*, the Garden Lounges were situated on the port and starboard side of the Smoking Room. The rooms had raised terraced floors. Flowers and plants were added to give the rooms a 'garden' feel.

Above: The main entrance hall, two decks high.

CINEMA—THEATRE

Another addition from the trip on board *Normandie* was the cinema. *Queen Mary* hadn't been built with one but the popularity of the *Normandie*'s was known. The cinema could hold 338 persons and the general colour scheme was red, white and blue – the seats were red, the walls an ivory colour and the carpet blue. The cinema was shared with cabin-class passengers (tourist-class passengers had a much more basic cinema of their own) and it had a small stage that could also be utilised for ship's concerts. During the post-war maiden voyage, someone managed to set the sprinkler system off during a film – unfortunately everyone was soaked and the cinema was flooded!

GYMNASIUM & SWIMMING POOL

The Gynmasium was on Sun Deck beside the Squash Courts and was fitted with the most up-to-date fitness equipment and also included old favourites such as horse- and camel-riding machines, boxing gloves, rowing machines, cycling machines and fencing foils.

The swimming pool was situated low in the ship on C deck. The room was 51ft long and 29ft in width and the swimming pool was 36ft long by 16ft wide. On the walls was a latex composition with mother of pearl chippings. The surface was interlaced with wavy metal strips of silver bronze.

The pool was finished with white briquettes and black nosing tiles, and the handrails and other fittings were of nickel alloy. The four columns at the side of the pool had a delicately shaded sea-green mosaic and the ceiling was painted white. It had dressing cubicles and shower baths at the fore end and Turkish and Curative Baths adjoining it. The

The gymnasium and swimming pool.

baths included a Frigidarium, Tepidarium, Massage Room, Vapour Room, Calidarium and Laconicum. In an age of innocence, different times were reserved for ladies and for gentlemen.

THE LIBRARY

The Library was off the Main Hall on the starboard side. The walls and furniture were treated with a horizontally inlaid veneer of canberil, and interspersed with this veneer were panels and window mullions of tulip burr. The bookcases were constructed with the same veneers and had concealed lighting as well as doors to stop the books falling out in rough weather.

Above: The *Queen Elizabeth* reaches New York on her second maiden voyage to be greeted by a multitude of boats and tugs. To the right can be seen a firefloat spraying fountains of water in celebration of this mighty ship.

<u>CUNARD WHITE STAR LIMITED.</u>

SPECIAL TRAIN

RESERVED SEATS   Date **25 JUN**   Time **11·15 an**

WATERLOO STATION, LONDON TO SOUTHAMPTON

connecting with Ship **QUEEN ELIZABETH**

YOUR SEAT IS IN ... CLASS RESERVED IN 23 COMPARTMENT No.	NUMBER OF SEATS RESERVED *three* INDICATED ON THE WINDOW OF THE COMPARTMENT

17/103.

CABIN. *A 168.*

SECOND SITTING.

Table No _____ **7** _____

Seat No _____ **3 & 4** _____

Name *Mr. Mrs. McLennan.*

Passengers are requested to hand this card to the Table
Steward when taking their seat at first meal.

37/8323

MRS McLELLAN'S VOYAGE

Collecting the material for this book has led the author to find certain small collections treasured over the years by the one-time traveller or tourist. As the slogan went, 'Getting there is Half the Fun' and people tended to treasure their mementoes of their trip. The following is just one such small collection of photographs and ephemera acquired from a Canadian estate and preserved for posterity. Mrs McLellan, the owner, was the wife of Captain R. D. McLellan, a war correspondent serving with the 3rd Canadian Public Relations Group attached to the Canadian Military Headquarters in London. As a member of the press, Capt. McLellan travelled to many countries throughout Continental Europe including France, Germany, Belgium and the Netherlands. When the war ended, Capt. McLellan was transferred to Germany as a correspondent with the Canadian Army Occupation Force.

While in Germany, Capt. McLellan became the exclusive Canadian distributor for diaries and photo albums manufactured by Richard Dohse & Sohn – a German firm.

The McLellans had for the time a wonderful lifestyle, travelling all over the world on famous ocean liners and staying at the most luxurious hotels. The couple wrote and spoke four languages fluently – English, French, German and Italian – and their hobbies included golf, tennis, theatre, opera, music, aquatic sports and animals. They had several cars including at least one Mercedes Benz, and an impressive collection of Ziess and Leica cameras.

Contained here is a record of Capt. and Mrs McLellan's voyage on the *Queen Elizabeth*. They took the Boat Train from Waterloo to Southampton on 25 June 1947 at 11.15 a.m. and sailed from Southampton that day.

Mrs. R. D. McLellan
NAME OF SHIP Q. Elizabeth
CLASS PASSENGER Cabin
DATE OF SAILING 25 Jun 47 ROOM No. C92/2
FROM (PORT) Southampton

OCEAN TERMINAL

During the 1950s a special terminal was built in Southampton to accommodate the Queens – Ocean Terminal. The Boat Train would run from Waterloo via Southampton en route to the dockside at Ocean Terminal where the passengers were transferred to the ship in luxury. In the reverse direction, they could clear customs in the terminal and then catch the train back to London. The terminal itself was huge, taking up almost the full length of the dock, but it was warm and comfortable, with shops such as a WH Smith and plenty of seating for the passengers and friends meeting them or seeing them off.

Unfortunately, the Ocean Terminal no longer stands in Southampton. After lying empty for a while it was demolished in the 1980s. Nothing stands on the site today and the loss of this fine building was such a shame. Its replacement, the Queen Elizabeth 2 Terminal, is further down the quay and was specially built to take the passengers of the *Queen Elizabeth 2*. A new cruise terminal has opened in the old Ocean Dock.

ACCIDENTS AND GROUNDINGS

Weather has always been one of the problems of transatlantic travel and Cunard ships have always been built to withstand the effects of even the stormiest weather. However, while accidents have happened in fog and rough weather, sometimes it is the unexpected in clear, calm conditions that has been the problem. It was rare to have an accident but when it happened to the largest ship in the world, the rest of the world knew about it. After a rough trip with high seas, the *Queen Elizabeth* arrived off Nab Tower, Isle of Wight, on 14 April 1947. Approaching Southampton, the weather had cleared up and now she was in sheltered waters – everything seemed to be fine. On approach she routinely picked up a pilot. This time the regular pilot, Captain Jim Bowyer, was on another ship and the next duty pilot came on board. The pilot that day was more accustomed to bringing in smaller ships and had never taken a Queen into Southampton before. Being less experienced he was unused to the handling and size of the largest ship in the world. While making an awkward starboard turn the *Elizabeth*, making about 3 knots, imperceptibly ran aground. This did not unduly worry Captain Ford as he knew the liner was in sheltered waters and that the bottom was a soft yellow clay, but it took over twenty-six hours and sixteen tugs before she was free of the mud.

Meanwhile, passengers felt they were kept in the dark about their predicament and the crew weren't informing them of what was going on. All outgoing radio communication was severed and passengers were unable to contact the outside world.

Much weight was lost by dumping thousands of tons of water and transferring most of the remaining fuel oil to a waiting tanker but the liner still stuck fast. A decision was made on 15 April that first-class passengers and their luggage should be disembarked by tender to help lighten the load of the ship. The first-class passengers and their luggage left at 4 p.m. All other passengers remained on board.

The *Elizabeth* was eventually pulled off the clay at 8.40 p.m. and unceremoniously pulled down the Solent stern-first. She was anchored 7 miles from Calshot because of thick mist and the passengers finally arrived at Southampton fifty hours after the grounding. Various inspections were made to the liner to check her seaworthiness. A 4-in rope had to be removed from one of her propellers. Later *Lloyd's Register of Shipping* surveyors ascertained the damage. Their report stated that there was a slight leakage from sprung rivets in one of the oil tanks and that traces of sand and shell were found in the four main condensers,

Above: Queen Elizabeth aground off the Isle of Wight and being rescued by six tugs. This was a rare accident to a Cunard Queen but, nevertheless, a very dangerous and costly one.

"Q

E"

R.M.S. QUEEN ELIZABETH

eight main lubricating oil coolers and four turbo-oil coolers. It was recommended that the ship go into dry dock for further investigation, but as there was no dry dock available at the time, it could be done at the next dry-docking.

Correspondence in *The Times* criticised the Cunard staff and the lack of information to passengers, many of whom had important business meetings delayed as a result of the incident. The grounding of the ship was front-page news in many newspapers and the potential loss to Britain's mercantile marine was huge. However, at the end of the day, all was well and the ship was safely refloated. For the next few years arguments continued over the navigation aids at Southampton, choice of pilot and costs incurred of salvage by tugs.

On 29 July 1959, the *Queen Elizabeth* had just departed Pier 90 in New York en route for Southampton. Meanwhile the United States Line

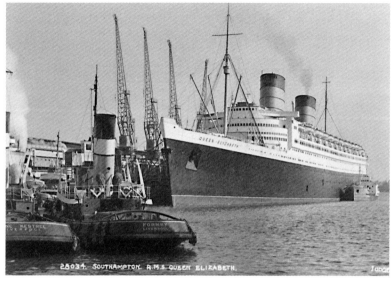

Above: At Southampton, *c.* 1955. (Courtesy of Judges of Hastings)

freighter *American Hunter* was just coming into port on a voyage from Le Havre. There was dense fog and, although both ships had radar, the two were on a collision course. The *Queen Elizabeth* was spotted off the *American Hunter*'s bow and a collision was inevitable. After the collision, the *American Hunter* was able to back off and then collided with a buoy. Both ships limped slowly to port and it was found that the *Queen Elizabeth* had been dented on her hull around the hawse pipe. Just below her anchor was a hole about 2ft in diameter. After a temporary repair using about 10 tons of cement, the *Queen Elizabeth* sailed for England that evening. The freighter reported a 2-ft dent, 20ft above the waterline.

An annual event was the refit in Southampton's King George V Graving Dock. Here *Queen Elizabeth* is seen entering the dock in 1952. The dry dock was built specifically for her and her sister by the Southern Railway and opened in 1933.

Above: Queen Elizabeth arrives at New York in the mid-1950s with, among others, *United States* and *America* already docked.

In the snow at Southampton.

Queen Elizabeth *Queen Mary*

BY FAR THE LARGEST SUPERLINERS IN THE WORLD

Cricket is played while the *Queen Elizabeth* is refitted at Southampton in 1946.

Refuelling on the turnaround at Southampton.

RMS *Queen Elizabeth* meets SS *America* off Cowes.

Being replenished at the Ocean Dock, Southampton.

A stunning view of the cruiser stern and the Ocean Terminal, built specially for the Queens. (Courtesy of Judges of Hastings)

Top: The American rival *United States* at Bremerhaven.

STRIKES

During their latter years, strikes were one of the main reasons for the downfall of the Queens. The *Elizabeth* and *Mary* were regarded as key ships in any dispute, and to stop them sailing would result in maximum chaos and publicity for the strikers' cause.

One strike ended with the *Queen Elizabeth*, *Queen Mary* and *Aquitania* sailing on the same day (2 December 1948) after lasting for sixteen days. This cost Cunard alone over £250,000 in lost revenue and expenses and caused much disruption to passenger travel. This strike was caused by longshoremen in the east coast of the United States. The crew members were in support and did not want to strike break, and the sailings were delayed as a solution to the strike was sought. To cut a long story short, after much negotiation the ship did sail but only after two strikes and a dense fog! Strikes on both sides of the Atlantic were becoming more common and every strike caused more people to travel by air. It was only a matter of time before traffic was in decline, much of it brought on by the strikers themselves.

A NEW SUPERLINER

Following the Second World War the government of the United States became increasingly disturbed by the lack of troop-carrying capacity on US-flagged ships. Britain and the other European powers had supplied most of the troopship capacity during the last war and the Americans did not want to have to rely on the British the next time. As a result of their experiences during the war, the American government decided to invest money in reviving the American merchant fleet and also decided to construct a new superliner. This new ship would be faster than any liner afloat and was able to be converted quickly into a troop carrier. Thus, the SS *United States* was born.

SS *United States* was launched in 1952 and could reach a speed of 38.25 knots. This new greyhound quickly took the Blue Riband from the *Queen Mary*. The *United States* was suddenly *the* ship to be seen on.

Queen Elizabeth floodlit at night in Southampton Docks in 1946, just prior to her maiden post-war voyage.

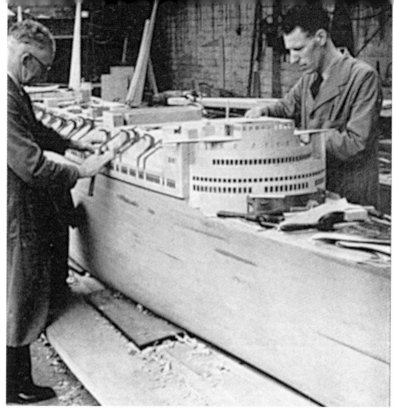

Cunard commissioned Bassett-Lowke, the famous Northampton model makers, to build a scale model of the ship. They had already supplied two similar models of *Queen Mary*. This model was destined for New York and was made from wood, weighed over 1½ tons and was beautifully crafted to be an exact replica of the original. The model was constructed from a single 6-ton log of African white mahogany, which was subjected to a fifty-six-day kilning process during which 110 gallons of moisture were extracted. Eight months and 6,900 man-hours transformed the tree trunk into the model shown here.

The hull was given twenty coats of paint, and hull markings were all hand painted. The model was transported to the New York offices of Cunard on board the *Parthia*, from Liverpool, in February 1949. Here she is seen being gently manouvered into the New York offices where she joined a similar 1/48 scale model of the *Queen Mary* that had resided here since 1936.

THE DOWNFALL OF THE QUEENS

Before the Second World War the long-range aeroplane was still in its infancy but, during the war, technological progress was rapid. By the end of the war, aircraft were flying between Britain and America on a daily basis. Regular travellers were impressed by this new method of travel. Although comfort was a lot more basic than on a ship, the fact that either America or Europe could be reached in a matter of hours, not days, was enticing. As aeroplane travel became more popular in the late 1950s and early 1960s, the Queens grew more like ghost ships. The advent of jets was the final straw, London to New York was a seven-hour journey instead of four or five days by sea.

This page: 9 August 1961 and the *Queen Elizabeth* departs Pier 90 at New York for another voyage to England. At New York, there was a thirty-six-hour turnaround before the return voyage. In that time passengers and their sometimes extensive luggage had to be disembarked, any repairs undertaken, the ship had to be replenished with food, refuelled with both oil and fresh water and a new set of passengers had to be embarked for England.

The photographs on this page were taken by a young Fulbright Travel Scholar named John Wilson, passionate about ships and lucky enough to visit the ship while she was in New York.

At Southampton's Ocean Terminal *c.* 1955. (Courtesy of Judges of Hastings)

At Cherbourg.

With the advent of the Jet Age and the downturn in passenger numbers, Cunard had two very large and expensive ships that needed some other use to remain profitable. The most obvious alternative use was cruising. While both ships and people had been cruising for the best part of one hundred years, its popularity in America increased with the 1930s 'Booze Cruises' to nowhere from alcohol-free America. The *Normandie* had been cruising twice to Rio during 1938 and 1939 and it seemed a logical thing to do. Cunard had even built *Caronia* in 1948 specifically for cruising. Cunard's four-stackers had also done their stints with both *Aquitania* and *Mauretania* going to the Mediterranean and to the Caribbean in the late 1920s and 1930s. But the question was – would this use suit the Queens? After all they were designed for one purpose only and they had shown signs of potential problems during their extended wartime travels. They were large ships that would be almost impossible to dock in smaller ports; they were designed for the cold North Atlantic, not the hot climates of the Mediterranean and Caribbean, and they didn't have the resources on board to carry more than about six days of essential supplies without replenishment. Cruising in the winter and transatlantic trips in the busy summer months was thought to be the Queens' saviour.

It was thought by Cunard management that the Queens would be a popular choice for cruising, especially as it was felt that many Americans had an affinity with the ships, having travelled on them during the war. These ex-GIs and many British ex-patriots were now making their fortunes in post-war America, and many would want their families to see the ship they travelled on during or just after the war.

At the beginning of the 1960s the *Queen Elizabeth* was sent up to the Clyde for a refit. Here she was transformed and given a new lease of life. An outdoor swimming pool was added, as was air conditioning, a lido deck and a laundry. She was generally spruced up ready for her

ABSTRACT OF THE LOG OF

R.M.S. "QUEEN ELIZABETH"

Commodore F. G. WATTS, R.D., R.N.R.

NASSAU NEW YEAR CRUISE 1964/65

Dec. 1964	Distance	Latitude N.	Long. W.	Weather, etc.
Tues. 29				At 16.01 EST (2101 GMT) left Pier 92, New York
				At 18.00 EST (23.00 GMT) A.C.L.V.—DEPARTURE
Wed. 30	479	32.36	75.24	Mod. W'ly breeze, mod. sea and swell. Partly cloudy
Thurs. 31	462	to arrival		At 06.15 Local Time (11.15 GMT)—ARRIVAL Nassau
	941	miles		At 06.39 Local Time (11.39 GMT) at Anchor

PASSAGE, New York to Nassau—1 day, 12 hours, 15 minutes

Steaming Time—1 day, 12 hours, 15 minutes.   Detention—Nil

Reduced Speed—36 hours, 15 minutes.   Average Speed—25.96 knots

Jan. 1965	Distance	Latitude N.	Long. W.	Weather, etc.
Friday, 1				At 17.30 LT (22.30 GMT) Anchor Aweigh
				At 17.42 LT (22.42 GMT)—DEPARTURE Nassau
Sat. 2	488	33.03	75.23	Fresh SW'ly breeze, mod. sea and swell, cloudy and clear
Sunday, 3	453	to arrival		At 08.12 EST (13.12 GMT) ACLV abeam.—ARRIVAL
	941	miles		

PASSAGE, Nassau to New York—1 day, 14 hours, 30, minutes

Steaming Time—1 day, 14 hours, 30 minutes   Detention—Nil

Reduced Speed—38 hours, 30 minutes   Average Speed 24.44 knots

---

R.M.S. 'Queen Elizabeth'   Cunard Line

Cruise Director Harold Grimes

and

Staff Purser W. D. Rouse

present their compliments and request

the pleasure of your company in the

Restaurant Cocktail Bar, "R" Deck,

at 7.30 this evening

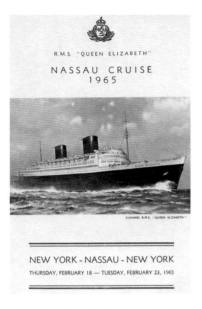

R.M.S. "QUEEN ELIZABETH"

NASSAU CRUISE
1965

CUNARD R.M.S. "QUEEN ELIZABETH"

NEW YORK - NASSAU - NEW YORK
THURSDAY, FEBRUARY 18 — TUESDAY, FEBRUARY 23, 1965

CUNARD

A view almost twenty years earlier than the picture opposite as she prepares to sail to Southampton on her coastal cruise of 1946.

potential new career. In the winter of 1962, the *Queen Elizabeth* made her first voyage as a cruise ship between New York and Nassau. Trips to the Bahamas were within her capabilities and range – she could be supplied with fresh water at Nassau and could carry enough fuel for a return trip. This was the first of three cruises during her winter break from the North Atlantic. Her passenger capacity was reduced from the 2,200 of a normal transatlantic voyage to between 1,000 and 1,300. In addition to her normal crew she also carried a Cruise Director and a team of Social Directresses. These additional members took charge of the special passenger activities on board the ship. After the success of the first trip, the scene was set for the *Lizzie* and the *Mary* to alternate between cruising and transatlantic service, with the *Mary* cruising to Las Palmas and the *Lizzie* spending most of her time cruising to Nassau, although she did complete a Mediterranean cruise in 1964.

Unfortunately, Cunard did not find the Queens as big a success as they had imagined; they were just too large for cruising and, with the competition of jet travel, unprofitable as transatlantic liners. They often ran as ghost ships with waiters and stewards outnumbering the diners in the restaurants. All but a few of their old passengers had deserted them for the speed and convenience of the aeroplane. Cunard began to look at a replacement for the *Queen Mary* in the late 1950s – she was over twenty years old and looking more than a bit dated. The idea of a new liner was born. Q3 was her code name (the third Queen liner). Things started getting serious in 1960 and discussions were held with the government to loan some of the money for construction. She was to be 75,000 tons, 990ft long and 114ft wide. Construction was planned to be by a Tyneside consortium but that was as far as things got. The plans were dropped. The market was changing and the new ship was never to go beyond the drawing board.

At the Cloch lighthouse after one of her refits in the 1960s.

She was fitted in the 1960s with an outdoor swimming pool on the lido deck in preparation for cruising.

Promenade Deck.

The Cocktail Bar in the early 1960s.

After careful consideration, the company decided it still needed a new liner to replace the two Queens. Q4 would be smaller than the *Mary* and *Lizzie* but she was designed from the outset to be a dual-purpose ship, as happy on the North Atlantic as in some exotic port. This design managed to get beyond the drawing board and the keel of Q4 was laid in June 1965 at John Brown's.

As the new liner was being constructed, the Queens were still making huge losses and it was decided to sell both before they haemorrhaged the company's finances. Sir Basil Smallpeice, Chairman of Cunard, announced that the *Queen Mary* would be withdrawn from service in 1967 (almost at the end of her natural life) and the *Queen Elizabeth* in 1968, despite her still having ten years of life after an expensive and extensive refit only two years before.

SALE OF THE QUEENS

As planned, the first to go was the *Queen Mary*. She made her last voyage for Cunard in late 1967, just as the new Q4 – the *Queen Elizabeth 2* – was being launched. Sold to the City of Long Beach, California, to become a museum, hotel and conference centre, she still remains there today as the only large monument to the great days of ocean liner travel.

As for the *Elizabeth*, her sale was less easy. She was still genuinely a useful proposition as a liner. Her life had been extended by ten years after the 1966 refit, but Cunard didn't want to sell her to a potential competitor. Ideally she was to go for a similar use as the previous year's *Queen Mary*. Various parties expressed interest, including Revd Billy Graham, the American Evangelist, who wanted to turn her into a Bible school. Countries as far away as Japan and Mexico showed an interest in her too. A suggestion was even made that she be purchased by Britain as a tourist attraction and maritime museum to be based in

**CUNARD LINE
5-DAY
EASTER
CRUISE TO
Bermuda
ON THE
AIR-CONDITIONED
QUEEN
ELIZABETH
SAILING FROM
NEW YORK
APRIL 7, 1966**

Southampton, but Britain could not afford such an extravagance. Long Beach had the benefit of millions of dollars of oil revenue to pay for their Queen. Britain was in the middle of devaluing its currency. There was no chance she would stay in Southampton.

An Expedition to Delaware

On 5 April 1968 Cunard announced the high bidder for the *Queen Elizabeth*. It was a consortium of Philadelphia businessmen – Mr Robert

Cunard staff load passengers' suitcases during a stevedore's strike at Southampton in May 1967.

Miller, Mr Charles Williard and Mr Stanton Miller. Their proposal was to dock the *Queen Elizabeth* in the Delaware River as the centrepiece of a venture featuring the Seven Wonders of the World, with *Queen Elizabeth* being the eighth! The consortium ran into problems when it transpired that the Delaware River was too shallow to take the *Elizabeth*. Financial cuts had also delayed the construction of the new highway to the site by four or five years. The consortium changed tack and now set their hearts on Philadelphia. Talks fell through and the ship was sold to interests in Florida instead.

The Port Everglades Authority and the Governor of Florida were enthusiastic about the new arrival. The preliminary plans were laid for a leisure complex to be built around her with tennis courts, golf course, monorail system, and an international village. There was also talk of convention facilities and a wedding chapel.

Her last voyage in Cunard service was in November 1968. After her final trip the *Lizzie* set sail for Florida. Within six months, the venture in Fort Lauderdale ran short of money and the Cunard company helped to bail the owners out – after all, the ship still hadn't been paid for. For Cunard it also seemed like a good investment opportunity. In October 1968, the Elizabeth (Cunard) Corporation of Florida was born. Cunard invested £1,000,000 to retain 85 per cent ownership of the vessel for a period of ten years and worked out a new financial deal with the consortium for the preservation of the *Elizabeth* as she was now known.

However, just before she left for the palm trees of Florida, she had one more special visitor. After the liner's last transatlantic voyage, Her Majesty Queen Elizabeth, The Queen Mother, came to say farewell to the ship named after her. Having been rundown and neglected for a long time, rust streaked down the white paintwork and the funnels. This was quickly spruced up for the Queen Mother's visit. At least it was on the port side. Starboard didn't get painted at all. After all it wasn't worth

At Cherbourg in the mid-1960s.

This page: Crowds watch the *Queen Elizabeth* leave on a voyage in the early 1960s.

it and the Queen Mother wouldn't see that side anyway. The *Queen Elizabeth* left Southampton on 28 November 1968. Her leaving was in stark contrast to the departure of the *Queen Mary* the previous year and probably represented attitudes to the ship in Britain. The *Elizabeth* quietly slipped out of her berth and left Britain's shores for the last time. Apart from the Albion Band of Southampton, there were very few well-wishers on the quayside to see her off. Unfortunately, due to an electrical fault with her whistle control gear, she wasn't able to respond to the whistles given by other ships in the area on her departure. This only added to the ill-feeling surrounding this sad occasion.

The *Elizabeth* was empty apart from essential crew as she ploughed the Atlantic waves to Fort Lauderdale. She was due to make landfall on 7 December and the police and coastguard were predicting 'Queen Fever'.

When the *Queen Mary* arrived at Long Beach, the highways were blocked and a huge flotilla of small boats surrounded the massive liner to welcome her to her new home and the same was expected of the *Lizzie*.

When she arrived off the Florida coast the planned route had to be abandoned because dredging work had not yet finished at her berth and was expected to take another twenty-four hours. James Nall, President of the Investment Corporation of Florida, contacted Commodore Marr and suggested that the ship cruise the Florida coast to Key Biscayne, a distance of 70 miles. This was a stroke of genius because it gave the Elizabeth Corporation extra publicity. The *Elizabeth* arrived the following morning and was put into a temporary berth until her own was ready. Thousands of well-wishers and a band of small boats came to welcome the ship.

This page: The first of the two greatest Cunard liners to depart from Britain and the North Atlantic forever was the *Queen Mary*, seen here leaving on her 'Last Great Voyage' from Southampton to Long Beach. On board were some London double-decker buses and one of the attractions of sailing round Cape Horn was to travel in a double-decker bus.

The paying off pennant was 300ft long, representing 10ft for every year of service.

Queen Mary in dry dock at Long Beach, before being prepared for conversion into a hotel and tourist complex.

The last Cunard timetable for the *Queen Elizabeth* with, appropriately, a view of her steaming away from the camera. Her lido deck swimming pool is clearly visible here.

The reverse of the same timetable. *Queen Elizabeth* was to last until November of 1968 before she departed for America to be a tourist attraction in Florida.

It was not long before the *Queen Elizabeth*'s troubles started again. After a 1968 election there was a change in the Port Everglades Commissioners and the new Commissioners felt uneasy about the whole project. They started to ask awkward questions and local newspapers became involved. The docks at Port Everglades were being rapidly expanded and the *Queen Elizabeth* was taking up some very expensive and useful real estate. After delicate, but inconclusive negotiations, it was decided that the tours of the *Elizabeth* should continue but only if they did not disrupt the normal business of the port. The Commissioners also claimed 10 per cent of admission and car parking. Finally, the liner was bringing in some revenue, but still not enough to maintain her as a premier attraction.

Another nail in the coffin for the venture was the curiosity of the press towards the background of the Elizabeth consortium members. The press reported links with the Mafia and the Teamsters Union. After investigations and surveillance by various government agencies, it was found that there were no Mafia links but that there was a close enough link with the Teamsters Union to arouse suspicion of financial irregularities.

As problems escalated in Fort Lauderdale, Cunard decided to sell the *Queen Elizabeth* again. After all, they owned 85 per cent of the company that owned the *Elizabeth* and it was in the interests of their shareholders to maximise the return from the ship. There was a great danger of the company in Florida going bankrupt. Various parties from all over the world sent sealed bids in for the ship. The highest bidder was

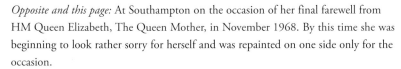

Opposite and this page: At Southampton on the occasion of her final farewell from HM Queen Elizabeth, The Queen Mother, in November 1968. By this time she was beginning to look rather sorry for herself and was repainted on one side only for the occasion.

an American consortium called Queen Ltd, which was a wholly owned subsidiary of the Utilities Leasing Corporation. There was a strange feeling of *déjà vu* as its shareholders included Stanton Miller, Robert Miller and Charles Williard. The consortium would pay $8.6 million for the *Queen Elizabeth*. She would remain at Port Everglades, and ambitious new plans had been drawn up for her future use. These included a 1,000-room hotel, maritime museum, cinemas, shops, an outdoor concert hall, eleven bars and seven restaurants. The additional area around the *Queen* would be used as a turning basin for cruise ships, a condominium complex and a marina. Even a chocolate factory was a possibility! The land required would be reclaimed from a mangrove swamp nearby.

These plans were a gamble which looked likely to pay off, except that the Securities Exchange Commission were in no hurry to approve the stock offer and the company went bankrupt in May 1969. Queen Ltd left debts of $12 million and most of this was to Cunard and the Utilities Leasing Corporation. The consortium tried one last time to save the liner, taking out an ad in the local newspaper, asking for the citizens of Fort Lauderdale to help them save her and also stating that various companies and individuals were persecuting them. But no support was forthcoming. The company was put in the hands of the receiver.

On 9 September 1970 a two-day sale was arranged at the Galt Ocean Mile Hotel in Fort Lauderdale. The receiver was allowed to sell the liner and all its contents to a reputable buyer. If this happened quickly it would reduce the bad debts incurring. There were 800 lots including the gymnasium, tables and chairs, curtains, paintings, crystal, and two galleys. In addition, the contents of the captain's cabin and the bridge were sold.

SALUTE to R.M.S. "QUEEN ELIZABETH"
(the world's largest liner)

HOMEWARD BOUND FROM NEW YORK ON HER
last Transatlantic Crossing to Southampton via Cherbourg
WEDNESDAY, OCTOBER 30 to MONDAY, NOVEMBER 4, 1968

THE QUEEN ELIZABETH IS SOLD

Mr Isidore Ostroff, acting on behalf of Mr C. Y. Tung of Hong Kong and Taipei, put forward an offer of $3.2 million for the ship and its contents, which was accepted. C. Y. Tung was a ship-lover, who owned one of the biggest shipping fleets in the world. He had a dream of converting the ship to an educational cruise liner – and this dream was to be called the *Seawise University*. Tung aimed to keep the *Queen Elizabeth* sailing and hoped that cruises around the world would help in promoting the mutual understanding and exchange in culture between East and West. The *Seawise University* would be on charter to the Chapman College of Orange in California and would carry 1,800 students and 800 cruise staff. The 'Seawise' name was even a clever play on C. Y. Tung's own name.

For the journey from Port Everglades to Hong Kong, he appointed Commodore Geoffrey Marr and Mr R. E. Philip (former Chief

Engineer of the *Queen Elizabeth*) to join the C. Y. Tung Organisation as Technical Advisers, with William Hsuan as Captain and W. C. Ceng as Chief Engineer. A Chinese crew was flown out to take the ship back to Hong Kong. After her years of neglect it took three months to prepare the new *Seawise University* and her engines for the voyage.

The *Seawise* left Port Everglades on 10 February 1971, with the crew little knowing she would never return. After one of her six working boilers developed a leak, she slowly edged her way towards the harbour entrance. She made her way out and towards the open sea. Then she had a serious malfunction with the remaining boilers, causing her to become powerless without the ability to steer or maintain speed. She was effectively helpless and it was decided to tow her to Aruba. After problems with drifting, the *Seawise* was taken in tow to an anchorage 6 miles from Oranjestad, Aruba. C. Y. Tung flew men and equipment to Aruba to repair the ship. Many boiler tubes were replaced and the ship prepared properly for a long sea voyage, all of this taking two months.

Fresh water and fuel were taken on at Curaçao and another similar stop was made at Trinidad. Rio de Janeiro was the *Seawise*'s next port of call on 30 May 1971 and then at Singapore on 7 July. She arrived in Hong Kong on 14 July and had to steam around for twenty-four hours as her welcome party had been arranged for the following day. The next day she was welcomed into Hong Kong harbour with helicopters, a flotilla of small boats and a fire boat display.

During the following months, C. Y. Tung reconditioned the *Seawise University*. Two thousand men were shipped daily to the liner, and her four engines overhauled and her twelve boilers properly reconditioned. She had also been painted in the white hull and orange funnels of Orient Overseas Line. She was even brought up to IMCO firefighting standards – which Cunard couldn't afford to do. She was then due to be dry-docked

*✻

Commodore's Dinner

FINAL NORTH ATLANTIC WESTBOUND CROSSING
SUNDAY, OCTOBER 27, 1968

—◦—

A Toast to the Queen Elizabeth

As this final Atlantic voyage draws to a close, we remember the many happy occasions and the many good friends we have known during this ship's 494 voyages.

We invite you to join us in "Saluting the World's Largest Passenger Liner" in wishing her a "Long and Happy Retirement," and in toasting the success of "Queen Elizabeth 2" which will follow her on the Atlantic next year.

[signature] DSC RD

Commodore

MENU

Chilled Melon Ball Cocktail with Crème de Menthe
Helford Oysters with Crèole Relish
Cornets of Smoked Salmon and Beluga Caviare

Clear Turtle Soup with Bristol Sherry (Chester Cheese Straws)
Cream of Chicken with Sorrel (Profiteroles and Quenelles)

Glazed Fillets of Dover Sole, Waleska

Boned Breast of Guinea Hen with Ham Lucullus

Grilled Mignon of Tenderloin — London House

Grand Marnier, Sorbet

Roast Prime Ribs and Sirloin of Angus Beef, Horseradish Cream

French Asparagus Spears, Mousseline
Green Sliced Beans, Amandine
Baked Idaho Potatoes with Sour Cream and Chives
Allumette Potatoes

Suprême of Florida Grapefruit and Avocado
Belgian Endive and Escarole Salad
Roquefort, Thousand Islands and French Dressings

Peaches Flambé in Kirschwasser   Rûche "Queen Elizabeth"

Jamaica Rum Soufflé

Selected Petits Fours

Fresh Fruit Basket   Coffee

Champagne

To Mr S. Banfield Chief Confectioner.

With Kindest Regards & Best Wishes for the Future. In Grateful Appreciation of many superb & Beautifully presented Sweets, that have had a disastrous effect on my waistline.

Thompson DSC RD
Commodore

RMS "Queen Elizabeth" on her Final Atlantic Crossing Nov 2nd 1968

in Japan to have her hull checked and painted. Great plans were made and much publicity issued promoting her forthcoming cruises.

There was clear sunshine on the morning of 9 January 1972. Around 540 workmen were aboard the *Seawise* continuing the conversion work, as the rest had gone for lunch. Completion was almost in sight and much of the work was on finishing touches. She was resplendent in her new colours and was beginning to look like a Queen once more. That morning the catering staff on board had been preparing for a reception that was being held later in the day by C. H. Tung, C. Y. Tung's son.

Then, someone noticed smoke! It was the very eve of her departure for Japan, everything had been done and all that remained was tidying up, painting and other small touches. She was set for her first fare-carrying voyage in almost four years, a seventy-five-day Circle Pacific cruise from Los Angeles starting on 24 April 1972.

At least four fires had been lit simultaneously around the ship. Many vents, hatches and doors were open and the flames were fanned by the air coming into the liner through these openings. The ship's fire crew had been aware of one blaze, but did not know about the others and while fighting one fire the others had time to get hold before they were noticed. The ship's crew and the guests at the reception on board were ordered to abandon ship. An hour after the fires had started, firefighting tugs arrived to pump water into the ship in a vain attempt to put them out. Full of precious woods and furnishings, the *Seawise* was a firetrap. The fixtures just helped fuel the flames. Attempts were made in vain to control the blaze, but after four hours, the *Lizzie* was abandoned and left to burn herself out. The water pumped on board caused the ship to list and she slowly keeled over. In a repeat of the final hours of the *Normandie*, the *Seawise University* eventually rolled on to her side with the weight of water and lay capsized on the seabed. Lying at an angle, smoke still pouring from her decks and out of every opening, she continued to throw a pall over Hong Kong harbour for days. She was once more international news. Headlines appeared in every newspaper. TV and radio covered her final hours as she succumbed to the smoke, flames and thousands of tons of water. One man's dream and months of work literally disappeared in a puff of smoke. Later a Court of Inquiry assessed that arson was probably to blame for the demise of this great liner.

Meanwhile the *Seawise* was left in Hong Kong harbour to rust. One year later, Commander Sir Ivan Thompson, and a group of men held a memorial service for her on Pier 90 in New York. While still *in situ* she was used during the film of the James Bond movie *The Man with the Golden Gun*. Headquarters of the British Secret Service were supposedly built into the wreck.

The launching of a ship is like the inception of a great human enterprise, an act of faith. We cannot foretell the future but in preparing for it we show our trust in Divine Providence. We proclaim our belief that by the grace of God and by man's patience and goodwill order may yet be brought out of confusion, and peace out of turmoil. With that hope and prayer in our hearts, we send forth on her mission this noble ship.

— H.M. The Queen (The Queen Mother) at the launch of the "Queen Elizabeth"

R.M.S. "QUEEN ELIZABETH"
(83,000 TONS)
1940 — 1968

This page and previous page: Views of the *Queen Elizabeth* as she approached the end of her life.

COME ABOARD

the ELIZABETH

QUEEN OF THE SEAS

The largest
ocean liner
the world
has ever seen

Sunshine State Prkwy.

I-95 | Rt. 84 | Andrews Ave. | U.S. 1

Eller Dr. N-Bound Ent. | S-Bound Ent. 28th St. | 24th St. | 17th St. Causeway

N→

17th St. & 24th St. gates
closed to tour traffic

14th

Sliphead Rd.

A.1.A.

Beach

This page: She was
to become a tourist
attraction in Florida
and is shown
arriving there.

This page and next page: Q4, better known as *Queen Elizabeth 2.*

Top left: On the same slip as her predecessors; most of the ship was built in prefabricated sections and then welded together.

Top right: A propeller.

R.M.S. Carmania   Cunard Line

20th September, 1967

Launching of

R.M.S. Queen Elizabeth II

Captain H. A. Stonehouse, D.S.C.*, R.D.,
R.N.R. (Rtd.)

invites you to partake of a glass of

champagne to toast the new ship.

She was fitted with stabilisers from new.

On the slip at John Brown's, ready for launching.

Announcing
the Maiden Voyage of SEAWISE
(formerly the R.M.S. Queen Elizabeth)
75-day Circle Pacific Cruise.

'It's the rebirth of a legend.'
After three years in retirement the former
R.M.S. Queen Elizabeth sails on an adventure-
filled Circle Pacific Cruise. Her name is now
SEAWISE UNIVERSITY. And she'll carry up to
1,400 first class passengers.

ELIZABETH – *Queen of the Seas*

Above: Her time at Port Everglades was to be short. Here she is surrounded by an almost empty car park.

Above left and below left: She was bought by C. Y. Tung and he began to convert her into the world's largest cruise ship.

After oil tanks ruptured, booms were set up around the ship and the decision to scrap her was taken, as salvage and repair, while perhaps possible, was uneconomic. Over a two-year period workmen and divers scrambled over the wreck, cutting her up into manageable sections, and recovering the brass and bronze and other valuable metals and alloys from the ship. The salvage company removed much of the liner down to the keel, which was abandoned in 50ft of water.

Outside the New York Offices of Orient Overseas Line, Mayor Lindsay unveiled a memorial to the ship. The granite memorial was made up of the letters 'Q' and 'E' and there were carved copies of letters from the Queen Mother and the Secretary General of the United Nations. It was a sad end to one of the finest ocean liners ever designed. The *Queen Elizabeth* was, for many years, the largest liner afloat and is still technically the largest true ocean liner ever built. Many modern cruise vessels are larger but few have the ability to stand up to the rigours of a Force 10 in the mid-Atlantic.

As *Seawise University* she sailed from Florida to Hong Kong, where she was to be refitted and converted to cruising with a maiden cruise in April of 1972.

An artist's impression of her in her Orient Overseas Cruises livery from a 1972 brochure advertising her maiden cruise for O.O.C.

FIRE SWEEPS LINER 'QE1' IN HONGKONG

Capsize fear after 20 hr. inferno

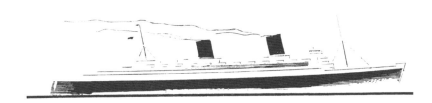

Opposite page: Seawise University on fire in Hong Kong harbour, just one day before her refit was to be completed in January 1972.

The burnt-out remains of the largest liner in the world. It was two years before she was cut up and removed.

The Queen Elizabeth burnt out in Hongkong

THE FUTURE

Although the *Queen Elizabeth* has gone and the *Queen Mary* is a tourist attraction at Long Beach, they have been replaced by one of the most famous liners to sail. The *Queen Elizabeth 2* has been an equal to her illustrious older sisters. She has served in war, being used as a troopship, and she is still the only liner making regular transatlantic sailings. Built in the same shipyard, she has already survived in service for longer than either of the Queens. Cunard itself is no longer British, having been through numerous owners. It now belongs to the Carnival Corporation, the world's largest cruise line, which is building a new cruise terminal beside the *Queen Mary* in Long Beach, California. It will soon be possible for travellers to leave on their vacation from a site next to one of the three great Cunard Queens. Meanwhile, in France, a new *Queen Mary 2* is being built and is due for completion in 2003/2004. The great Queens still live on!

Above: Queen meets Queen. *Queen Mary 2* arrives at the Carnival cruise terminal, Long Beach.

Left: *Queen Mary 2* evoking the classic Art Deco bow shot.

Above: Queen Mary 2 and *Queen Elizabeth 2*, New York.

Above right: Queen Mary 2 berthing at Liverpool.

Right: Queen Mary 2 arrives in San Francisco.

Above left: Meeting of *Queen Victoria* and *Queen Mary 2* at Sydney.

Above: Fireworks, *Queen Victoria*.

Left: Queen Victoria on her sea trials.

Opposite page: Cunard's latest liner, *Queen Elizabeth*, in Venice's lagoon.

Overleaf: HM Queen Elizabeth names Cunard's *Queen Elizabeth* at Southampton.

ACKNOWLEDGEMENTS

Like all books, this one would not have been possible without the help of numerous other people who have helped with information, photographs and support while the book has taken shape. I'd especially like to thank Dr John Wilson for providing a variety of photographs and pieces of ephemera from his extensive collection as well as for reading through the text.

Judges of Hastings should also be thanked for allowing me to use a couple of their photographs of the *Queen Elizabeth* at Southampton as should Mr Peter Hall – a wonderful and kind person – who provided me with some of the photos of the *Queen Mary* leaving Southampton on her Last Great Cruise. I would like to thank Gian Rossignuolo as well for giving me so much information about Captain and Mrs McLellan.

Thanks are also due to Jackie Webb at Wotton Lawn Library, Gloucester, for use of the library and the peace and solitude this provided while I was working on the text. My husband, Campbell, has also kept my enthusiasm up while writing this book.

I would like to thank a few people at Cunard also, and they are: Michael Gallagher, of Cunard Line, for allowing me to use the images of the *Queen Mary 2*, *Queen Victoria* and the new *Queen Elizabeth*; and Captain Ronald Warwick and his wife, Kim – after feeling disillusioned and 'all at sea', Captain Warwick, Kim and the *QE2* gave me such inspiration and enthusiasm to complete the book, that I will be forever in their debt.